The Official Computer Widow's
(and Widower's)
Handbook

**By Experts on Computer
Widow/Widowerhood**

Editing by Tina Berke and Gretchen Lingham
Cover illustration by Randy Verougstraete
Inside illustrations by Lisa Mozzini and Doug TenNapel
Art direction by Kay Thorogood

First Edition Copyright© 1990
Computer Publishing Enterprises
P.O. Box 23478
San Diego, CA 92123

0-945776-15-2

CONTENTS

This book is dedicated to the unsung veterans of the Computer Revolution: those whose spouses have become addicted, obsessed, enthralled with, absorbed by and otherwise enamoured of computers.

INTRODUCTION

Losing Your Spouse:
A Guide to What Makes
the Obsessed Computer
User Tick

It's not the first time someone has lost their spouse. In the fall numerous spouses are lost to football, especially on Sundays and Monday nights. Many people have lost their spouse to other people. Some people lose their spouse to the spouse's job. But there is something insidious about losing your spouse to a computer.

Football only happens in the fall. The games are on for a limited time with lots of commercials giving you time to bug your spouse. Computers have no seasons, time limits or time-outs for commercial messages. When you lose your spouse to a computer, you may never talk to him or her again. Yeah, you'll get to see the nerd . . . peering intensely into the computer screen—which in turn casts morbid shadows onto the user's face while an eerie feeling of despair and loneliness pervades your being.

When you lose your spouse to another person it is emotionally devastating, but at least you can, and probably will, do something about it. You can get a divorce and look for someone else, feeling fully vindicated in your decision. You can take a gun and blow his or her head off, then sit securely in jail for the rest of your life. Or maybe you can win your spouse back, when he or she tires (and they always do) of the little escapade.

But when you lose your spouse to a computer, nothing is on your side. Your spouse will tell you that the computer was purchased to make *you* rich—and use the same justification to sit in front of the stupid machine all day and night. (Of course, a laptop computer will be needed to take on vacations ... all to make *you* rich.)

If you file for a divorce, the entire world, including your own mother, will accuse you of standing in the way of the future of our society. They'll point out that you're being selfish and demanding.

If you shoot your spouse, you'll always wonder, while sitting in jail, whether your spouse might not have actually made *you* rich, given the chance.

Don't think of winning your spouse back from the computer, because there are three million people out there writing programs for the machine just to keep your mate in front of it. You would be better off if your spouse *did* have an affair. ("At least you know where I am." Big deal!)

If you lost your spouse to the job, more income might actually be produced for you to use in creative ways of amusing yourself. But with a computer the job is brought home and used in ways that "are going to make money," but almost never do. Besides—if your spouse is at the office, you can always go out for a bite to eat or something. But if your spouse is at home on the computer, you will be expected to stay and keep him or her company. It's like holding a conversation with a Pet Rock.

It's a terrible thing, being a computer widow or widower ... eating Doritos every night for dinner, trying to cope with the loneliness of being with someone who is there in form only, unable to understand what has happened to all of your dreams.

Never fear—you are not alone.

Millions of computer widows and widowers realize it is time to solve this problem. This book is the first step toward organizing computer widows and widowers. Written especially to amuse and possibly help you in your hour of need, *The Computer Widow's (Widower's) Guide* is your start to a new life of excitement and contentment. (Who knows? Your spouse may even talk to you after you read this book.)

Chapter One features a complete guide to what makes the obsessive computer user (your spouse) tick. This psychological profile will help you understand the thoughts, emotions, habits and techniques for training of the obsessed computer user (your spouse). Armed with this knowledge, either you will be able to develop a better relationship with your spouse or do things that will drive your spouse to the funny farm (whichever you prefer).

In Chapter Two you will find techniques and approaches for dealing with the trauma of computer widowhood. Not all of the techniques are for everyone. You will have to select the ones which best fit your situation and adapt them to your needs. If none of these suggestions work, we suggest professional help, and we don't mean a hit man.

In Chapter Three we have a story, "Birth of a Computer Widow," by Stephanie Atlas, and a poem "Computer Widow— The Poem," by Maxine Edwards, two real live computer widows. These are included to help you see that there are truly others in the same boat. In fact, it's a pretty crowded boat.

Chapter Four is a romance aimed at computer widows. It serves as entertainment for those late nights when he or she is up and out of your life computing. Chapter Five is a mystery which will keep you on the edge of your bed (if it doesn't put you to sleep).

Chapter Six is a brainstorm of things you can do while your spouse is on the computer. When you are stuck, depressed and just plain fed up, check this chapter for salvation.

Chapter Seven is a collection of jokes about computer users (your spouse). Where it may not be legal to discriminate against people based on race, creed, color, sex, national origin, age or religion, you can discriminate against computer users. Some people claim that it is merely an alternate lifestyle, but we know better.

Chapter Eight, if you can stomach it, is a Computer Widow/Widower's Guide to Computers. This has been included for those of you who actually want to communicate with your spouse on a level that they can understand through the noise of crunching Doritos. It will also help you to ask your spouse embarrassing questions about their very own computer.

Chapter Nine complements Chapter Eight with a series of questions and answers by our resident expert, Digital Dave, that will actually help make sense of computers to anyone, including dogs and cats. When you sneak off to look up one of the many questions that pop up while watching your spouse use this stupid machine, you will actually be able to talk about it later in casual conversation ... with the dog, cat or another computer user.

Chapter Ten is an explanation of the new organization Computer Widow's/Widower's of America (CWWA). It details the purpose, mission, benefits and bylaws of CWWA and shows you how you can sign up. The disease called Computer widow/widowerhood is going to get worse before it gets better. Now is the time for CWWA!

If none of this has helped, there is still a special feature of this book that will aid any computer widow/widower with their spouse. The binding of this book has been designed with a unique formula which is guaranteed to get the attention of your computer addicted spouse when you sneak up behind him/her and rap him/her on the head with the bound edge (one of the best techniques developed for self-help books).

"I'm not sure I like your friends."

CHAPTER 1

*The Obsessed
Computer User:
A Psychological Profile
By Stephen R. Frederick, M.D.*

It has often been assumed that obsessed computer users are just like anyone else—with the same motivations, habits and inclinations as the average person. Research shows that this is not the case.

Studies indicate that the average Obsessed Computer User (OCU) is missing a gene on one chromosome, while having an extra gene on another. This has been found to be true on both male and female OCUs. There are a number of effects from this genetic variation which at first appear to be benign, but upon closer investigation are definitely peculiar, if not perverse.

The brain of an OCU is networked differently from the normal human. There appears to be an increased number of connections on the left side of the brain. In the center of these connections are a group of nerve endings and amino acid chains forming a vortex that leads to the subconscious. This is known as the Left Brain Drain, otherwise called the LBD.

Increased activity is noticed in this area of the brain when the OCU is in an intense algorithmic seizure which accompanies the use of a computer. It is theorized that the Left Brain Drain (LBD) is responsible for the almost-comatose state of the OCU when in contact with a computer.

Since the Left Brain Drain (LBD) is directly connected to the subconscious, over some period of time the seizures become the normal OCU state-of-mind—making it very difficult to communicate with the OCU. This is know as Hardening of the Algorithms (HA), or Programmer's Brain (PB).

There are a number of physiological, as well as emotional, symptoms associated with HA or PB. The first is a noticeable indentation on the right side of the skull from a lack of activity in the right brain. It appears that the right side of the brain actually atrophies, much the same as a right-handed tennis player's left arm will often dry up and fall off from a lack of use. This is one reason why juggling is becoming such a popular sport, while tennis is on the decline.

Another physical symptom of Hardening of the Algorithms (HA) is chapped lips. It has been found that large numbers of OCUs are addicted to Dorito Corn Chips (DCC). There appears to be a psycho-kinetic relationship between HA and the consumption of DCCs. The saline substance which adheres to the lips of the OCU after consumption of DCCs causes the licking of the lips; ergo: chapped lips—not at all uncommon.

OCUs with Programmer's Brain (PB) often have calluses on the end of their finger tips. This is from continuous interaction with a computer keyboard and the removal of salt from DCCs. As an early warning symptom, with new cases of PB the OCU will often have blisters before they actually form

into calluses. With some types of computers, most notably the Apple Macintosh (AM), the OCU will develop Mouse Finger (MF). MF is recognized by the callus forming on the index finger of the AMOCU. MF is found on the left index finger of the Left-handed AMOCU (LHAMOCU) and on the right index finger of the Right-handed AMOCU (RHAMOCU).

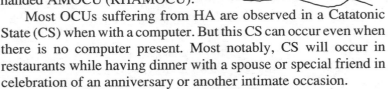

Most OCUs suffering from HA are observed in a Catatonic State (CS) when with a computer. But this CS can occur even when there is no computer present. Most notably, CS will occur in restaurants while having dinner with a spouse or special friend in celebration of an anniversary or another intimate occasion.

The OCU, who may have been attentive and responsive, will suddenly stare out the window and strike a rigid pose. The eyes will start to slowly wander and the head will rotate as if looking for something on the table. The OCU will then flash a pen out of the pocket and begin scribbling on the nearest napkin. It is at this time that the OCU will most often say, "Keep talking, Dear. I'm listening."

To the layman, a Catatonic State (CS) can be quite disconcerting, but rest assured that this is a perfectly normal occurrence for the OCU. What has actually happened is that the subconscious, which is directly connected to the left brain via the LBD, has just sent a signal that it has found the Lost Algorithm (LA). At this point it is very important for the OCU to permanently seize the LA before it gets away. This seizure can only be done by writing the LA down.

It is best to make sure the OCU always carries a writing utensil. Napkins will suffice as a medium for the inscription of the Lost Algorithm (LA), but it is not uncommon for the OCU to write on a tablecloth or even their own hand. Don't stand too close to an OCU during a CS. You may be written on.

You should be cautioned against trying to break the OCU out of a CS. This can be very dangerous and destructive. During the CS the OCU is looking for the LA and, at that time, nothing is more important then getting that LA. If the OCU is broken out of the CS and loses the LA, possibly forever, then the OCU will become frantic, despondent and angered. Your evening with the OCU is dead and if the LA was important enough, your relationship with the OCU may begin rapidly eroding for the long term. It is best to wait out the CS. It will usually pass in five to ten minutes and you will be able to continue on with a very pleasant evening. Many veteran spouses of OCUs will always carry a book with them to read whenever a CS occurs.

When a Catatonic State (CS) occurs while the OCU is using a computer, the natural clock of the OCU is frozen in place. In many cases it has been noted that the OCU's wristwatch may actually stop. This is called a Programmer's Brain Time Warp (PBTW). The OCU loses all sense of time. Hours fly by in what seems to the OCU like minutes. It has been theorized that during PBTW, the computer is actually sucking time out of the OCU. This would account for the OCU walking into the bedroom at four o'clock in the morning after almost 24 hours of a CS and saying, "When's lunch?"

On the emotional side, the OCU does not regard the computer as a machine. The OCU sees the computer as anthropomorphic: though not human, having numerous human qualities. This perverse attitude has been observed in many other forms of neurosis: most notably, the recently divorced 47-year-old male with regards to a newly purchased Corvette.

The OCU not only thinks of the computer as being human, but will actually develop a communication and dialogue with the computer. This is much more difficult, though not impossible, with a Corvette. The computer figuratively tells the OCU when something has been done well and literally tells the OCU when something has been done poorly. And the OCU never has to ask, "Was it good for you?" The OCU sees the computer as an undemanding companion with infinite patience. In the eyes of the OCU, the sole role of the computer is to serve and please the OCU. And the computer never complains. Is it any wonder that so many Computer Users (CUs) become OCUs?

An OCU with a computer is comparable to a teenager with a mirror. Everything the OCU sees in the computer is a reflection of the OCU. Intelligence, brilliance, creativity and ingenuity are all part of the reflection from a computer. Of course, the OCU will love the computer.

The basic rule of thumb when dealing with an OCU is never regard the computer as the enemy. If you try to attack the computer head on, you'll get creamed. The virtues imbued on computers by OCUs are far superior to any human virtues. It is impossible for any human to compete with a computer on an emotional level. Humans are selfish. Computers are not selfish. Humans are petty. Computers don't care enough to be petty. Humans demand more attention. Computers don't even care if you turn them on. See if you can find a human like that. You don't stand a chance.

You must regard the computer not as an enemy, but as a friend. The OCU must see that you do not feel threatened or intimated by the machine.

Use the same terms when referring to the computer as the OCU. This will help you to gain the trust of the OCU. OCUs are generally paranoid about anything concerning their computer. They feel that most people are planning to take their computer away. They fear losing their computers more than National Rifle Association (NRA) members fear their guns being taken away. OCUs will often chant slogans such as "Computers don't kill people, people kill people!" and "Computers are people, too!" If you can learn the same terms of endearment the OCU uses when talking about the computer, then you're way ahead of the game.

OCUs are obsessed with speed. Not with their own speed which, as a computer jogger, would not be all that great, but with the speed of the computer. Whether it is processor speed, RAM speed or disk speed, for the OCU, more is better. With the earlier, slower computers, there were often lulls in computing while the computer was compiling or processing. This made natural breaks in the Catatonic State (CS) when the OCU would travel to the kitchen for a cup of coffee or some light conversation. With growing technology and speed the breaks became fewer and shorter in duration—with many OCUs collapsing at the keyboard. This gives a new meaning to the phrase "speed kills."

Some OCUs tend to be obsessed with Tight Code (TC). TC has very few words and no embellishments. This accounts for OCUs being people of few words. They don't like to use adjectives and will often give the punch line without telling the joke. When giving direction to the lost, OCUs will usually just point.

Other OCUs may be just as dogmatic about the beauty of programming code. This is the Elegant Solution Syndrome (ESS). These OCUs have often found a particular Lost Algorithm (LA) that they dearly love. To them it is so beautiful that it must be used in every piece of programming, related or not. They take great pride in writing long programs which are completely indecipherable, yet still functional. These are the people who say, "Half the fun is getting there." OCUs suffering from ESS should never be put in the same room with OCUs obsessed with Tight Code (TC). They will kill each other.

To further understand the OCU it is necessary to understand how they think. Unlike most people, OCUs suffer from Linear Thinking (LT). This means that they can only think of one thought at a time and it must be in a logical sequence. If you are having a discussion with an OCU and you wish to change the subject, you must do it slowly. Otherwise, they will stay on the original subject. For example, if you want to change the conversation from Johnny's soccer game to new living room furniture the conversation should go something like this:

You: "Johnny needs a new soccer ball."

OCU: "What happened to the old one?"

You: "A car ran it over. There is a sports store with a sale on soccer balls."

OCU: "Oh? Where is this sports store?"

You: "You know, the one next to that furniture store."

OCU: "What furniture store?"

You: "The one that is having a sale on that new sofa we want."

OCU: "What sofa?"

You: "The one we discussed the other night at dinner."

Now, you have the OCU. The OCU knows that a CS occurred the other night, but doesn't remember a thing that was said. Guilt and Linear Thinking (LT) have brought you to this point. If you had not taken advantage of the OCU's LT, this is what may have happened:

You: "Johnny needs a new soccer ball."

OCU: "What happened to the old one?"

You: "A car ran it over. Maybe we can look at a new sofa while getting a new ball."

OCU: "What car ran over Johnny's soccer ball?"

You: "The neighbor's car. You know that we need a new sofa."
OCU: "What was the ball doing in the street?"
You: "Johnny kicked it there. We talked about the sofa at dinner the other night."
OCU: "I thought that Johnny wasn't allowed to kick the ball out front?"

The OCU just isn't getting the message because of Linear Thinking (LT). The OCU cannot change the course of conversation unless there is a logical link, no matter how obscure, to the new direction. Too many people mishandle OCUs by not accounting for LT.

It is easy to overlook LT because many OCUs will appear not to suffer from it. These OCUs will often completely change the subject in the middle of a conversation. This is merely an aberration of LT that will occasionally manifest itself. You may be discussing Johnny's soccer game with the OCU when the OCU will suddenly say, "I'm thinking of becoming a Buddhist." This does not appear to be consistent with LT, yet it is. The OCU is just Dropping a Bit (DB). When DB occurs, an amino acids chain has actually dropped out of one algorithmic network, falling through the Left Brain Drain (LBD), and landing on another algorithmic network, causing the violent change in direction—not at all uncommon.

This detailed and in-depth psychological profile is designed to help you better understand the inner workings and hidden mechanisms of your OCU. The research is continuing and it is expected that new discoveries will be made about OCUs and their deviant behavior. As of this writing there is no known cure and few treatments, but with enough time and government support and money, there probably never will be a cure for the Obsessed Computer User (OCU).

CHAPTER 2

Computer Widowhood
Survival Tactics
By Kay Thorogood

When you are outnumbered, it's not often you can win. I fought for my home, my space and my sanity. I lost not only the battle, but the war.

It was another day, another commute home from work. As I approached the driveway of my home, I squeezed my garage-door opener. As the door rose, I noticed that my half of the garage was strewn with empty computer boxes, foam pieces, plastic and paper. Parking inside the garage would be impossible. I parked on the street because my son's car occupied the middle of the driveway.

As I passed through the garage, I didn't bother to call out his name or greet him with a warm hello. I knew from past experience his mind was fully immersed in computerland and he wouldn't hear me anyway. I opened the back door and walked toward the kitchen, stepping over more boxes and computer parts scattered in the family room. I made my way through the kitchen to the living room, observing that even more computer objects were in the entryway.

I remarked to my husband later that evening that I had come a long way in accepting my family's interest in computers. There was a time when the entrance of one computer unnerved me. Now, I take in stride the loss of control of my home, the mess that comes with the computer and the attention my husband and two boys give to a manmade object.

I've analyzed the past ten years—from the very first day a computer planted itself in our home, to this very moment as I input this text into our PC. It's been a long, hard field to plow for me and in hindsight, I could have made my acceptance of the computer and my family's interest in the computer so much easier.

It occurs to me that I can share my pain, frustrations, anxieties, resistance and threatened position with other computer widows so that they might skip some of the agony I suffered. With my knowledge and wisdom, there should be no reason why a computer widow cannot co-exist in the same home with one or more computer nerds.

Sally and Fred seemed to have solved
their communication problem

I can tell you:

- What to do if you are outnumbered
- What you have to do to survive the takeover of your home
- Why you should believe up-front that the computer is permanent
- Why you should give up being threatened
- How your family will develop a sixth sense about you
- What will happen if you don't use the opportunity to learn from your knowledgeable group
- Why you shouldn't believe or trust your co-habitants
- What will happen if you make quick assumptions about computers
- Why you should accept new technology and dump the old
- Why you need to swallow your pride
- Why you should give up control of your child's destiny
- When and why you need to set limits

If you live by the widowhood survival rules set forth in this chapter, your life with a computer and its many extensions will make your existence in your home and on this planet simple, pleasant and peaceful.

It was in the early '80s that my husband, for some unfathomable reason, decided we needed a computer in our home. I reluctantly agreed, but there was one ironclad rule he had to agree to before a purehase could occur: The computer would not become a glorified toy.

Therefore, no games would be allowed except, of course, educational games. I had personally witnessed how bizarre a child can look and act when hooked into a video game at the local Seven/Eleven or video arcade, and no child of mine would turn into a mindless robot unable to respond to the slightest comment or instruction.

I could visualize both of my young boys hooked to this monster day in and day out, game after game. What happened to those days when they played with building blocks and Lego? How could I find the extra time to guard them against not only the violent or mindless TV programs but their possible addiction to computer games?

Naturally, they all agreed to my stipulation without hesitation. I was slightly concerned that I had won this argument so easily.

Much too easily.

My second concern was where this monstrosity, this eyesore, this ugly gray mass would be placed in my thoughtfully decorated and color-coordinated home. "The spare bedroom," they told me. "You mean my 'guest' bedroom, don't you?" I said, pointedly.

This room was all white with beautiful white walls, a lovingly handmade crocheted white bedspread from Grandma, eyelet shams and white wicker everywhere. I moaned and groaned and even whined a little in hopes that they would abandon this crazy idea. They assured me our old, brown, beat-up card table with that machine on top would not intrude or destroy my artful creation.

Sure!

I can't remember, and have probably purposely forgotten, exactly when "it" arrived. All I can remember on that first day was the maternal hovering of my husband and two boys over that gray box in the corner of the room. I was annoyed and uncomfortable to see the room transformed into a part office/guest room. What was the big deal about this machine, anyway? Why wasn't it in the garage with the tools, lawnmower and junk?

It was just a fancy typewriter or video game machine disguised as a computer. It wouldn't last, I assured myself, just like the Atari. It would be out of this place in no time. I would and could wait this one out patiently. My masterpiece would return to its former state of existence.

Well, weekends and months passed and the computer, ugly as ever, was still in the corner of my room. Even worse, every Saturday or Sunday two of them would sit on the edge of the bed (and the bedspread) watching the lucky one at the computer—with absolutely no regard for the delicacy of the treasure Grandma had made for me. I was proud of myself because I remained calm. I asked them to pull the spread back when they sat on the bed; I dragged in chairs and cushions for them.

Soon, the bed became a desk. Papers, disks and books were spread out. Homework was done on the floor to be close by in case a new happening arose with the computer. They politely but distantly nodded their heads at my every comment or instruction regarding the order and care of the room, barely noticing my presence.

I had seen that look before. It was the very same look every kid in front of a video game had in an arcade.

I just knew that they would sit on that bedspread if I wasn't nearby to protect it, and the walls would end up black and the pillows scrunched and the bedspread a sagging mess. I became obsessed with this room and the bedspread in particular. What about Grandma's legacy? Didn't it matter to them? They were dazed and I was crazed.

One day while they were at school and work, I took a long, hard look at this perfection of a room and realized that a year had passed and their enthusiasm had not diminished at all. In fact, it had escalated. I had become a prison guard with no authority. And my guest room hadn't been used once since the invasion of the creature. I came to the conclusion that it was time to give up the vigil that was causing me so much grief.

The rest of the house did not command my attention nearly as much as this room. It was definitely lived in, especially with two boys, a dog, a cat and a rat. No, I was not threatened, really. All I wanted was one special room undisturbed by any and all creations—especially one particular man-made creation.

But it was obvious the thing was here to stay. It finally occurred to me that my family really needed more room, a whole room, and that I was being selfish.

So, I sold the bed and furniture and packed away my precious heirlooms. No one seemed to be surprised by my first strange move. It was as though they thought it was inevitable. Nor was my husband surprised or amazed when I bought him a three-piece oak computer desk for Father's Day, or a printer for Christmas for all three of them, or a modem the following Christmas.

Yes, they seemed to take this all in stride. Did they know something I didn't?

After giving much thought to my year-long, excruciating experience, I came to a rude awakening. The computer was to reside with us on a permanent basis and I might as well accept the situation. I had to declare an armed truce. The computer had taken my family into custody and I had to decide whether to join them (unacceptable, yuk, forget it) or find positive aspects to my ordeal. I also sensed that this first realization would be part of a long string of realizations, and that I would be challenged to find creative ways to cohabitate with three star-struck human beings and one intruding machine.

I also recognized that in order to survive the upcoming life-long tribulation, I would have to live by a set of rules which could only be assigned after I experienced one ordeal at a time. I had endured a year of painful events and felt confident that I was qualified to put in place my first group of rules of widowhood survival, not only for my own well being, but for future generations of widows of America.

When I put pen to paper, I was startled to comprehend that I had learned so much in just one year:

Rule No. 1

If you are outnumbered in your home, you will lose every battle associated with a computer.

The larger the number in your family, the greater the probability they will gang up on you. Their forces are stronger. You are one against a very strong army. I can guarantee that you will not win one struggle unless you join their ranks.

They are very clever, too, in getting you to believe they are adhering to your requests, pleading, whining and fussing, when the opposite is actually happening. In reality, they have tuned you out and their words are just empty promises. It is fruitless to attempt to fend them off. Accept the inevitable.

Rule No. 2

The computer will become a permanent resident of your home. Believe the certainty of this law.

If you are confident that the computer is a temporary toy soon to be replaced by another diversion, make an appointment to have your head examined. The computer and its followers have other plans over which you have no control. Not only will it reside in your home, it will occupy a much bigger area then you anticipated. Its control will spread like wildfire.

Rule No. 3

If you think your home still belongs to you after the computer occupies a spot in it, you have a huge illusion to overcome.

Just because you decorate it, pay the house payment, clean it and maintain it endlessly doesn't mean you have any control over your home whatsoever. Your cohabitants seem to breath more than their fair share of air, occupy more priceless space then they could possibly use in a lifetime and manage to quietly commandeer your destiny with all the innocence of a newborn baby. The joke is on you. Give up total possession of your home and accept the unavoidable—it will never be the same as long as the computer is within close proximity of your property line.

Rule No. 4

You will feel threatened in the beginning when the computer enters your home, and you will also deny this emotion vehemently. Cave in now and greet it with open, loving arms.

Don't fight it. Find a room right away, set up a designated area immediately, shut the door. Throw in food from time to time. Even an occasional piece of software. Don't deny your feelings—because whether you want to or not, you will come around to adopting the idea that computers aren't so bad after all. I know, these words make you cringe with disbelief, but it will prove true.

Rule No. 5

Realize from the very onset that your dear loved ones know the eventual outcome of your overt or covert resistance long before you do. They have developed a sixth sense.

With this new gift of perception, they will determine far sooner than you ever imagined that your resistance to the computer will wear down. They will eventually get their way. They are persistent and patient because of their wisdom. No surprise will be exhibited when you have a change of heart—

Alice has found a use in the kitchen for the computer

they already knew you would cross over to their way of thinking. Give up, there is no hope. You've lost the battle before you've begun. You will gain peace of mind as a result.

In hindsight, it's hard to understand why I was so obssessed and irrational when the computer managed to find an important spot in our home and in the lives of my threesome. Computers do have a way of making an otherwise sane, mature, logical and sensible adult lose it.

Once I gave up my possessiveness of the guest room, I seemed to relax a bit when it came to our new member of the family. I think I felt like the displaced two-year-old when the parents bring home the newborn from the hospital. I was sure the computer would soon leave the premises, just as the two-year-old is certain that the baby sibling will leave the next day.

I grew accustomed to being left alone more and more as my family spent many intense hours trying to solve some strange glitch here and there. Gradually, I came to the realization that I had stumbled upon something that I had not had since childhood: freedom.

Ever since my threesome became so enthralled with their new buddy, I discovered that I could read a book at length without interruption, take a bath without all three plus the dog in the bathroom sharing their day with me, talk on the phone without asking them to turn down the volume on the TV, take a run or ride a bike without one or all of them wanting to tag along. In fact, they didn't even notice I was missing.

The more I thought about it, the more excited I became. In fact, I became downright ecstatic. I had actually discovered a newfound freedom I'd long since lost ... space.

Years of tending to babies and toddlers and maintaining togetherness as a family had taken their toll on me. Now, I could be by myself and not feel guilty. I could relax knowing that their father was interacting with them on a personal and intellectual basis. I reasoned that they were beyond wanting to do things with mom as in the past, like take walks to check out the local construction site, make Play-dough, have squirt-gun fights or roller skate. I could hardly contain myself with the joy of finding freedom after years and years of giving all my time to my young family and busy husband. Finally, I was given a gift of peace and time alone without interruption.

Rule No. 6

Don't overlook a glaring advantage of your widowhood state that might be staring you right in the face.

Too often, we want to control a situation whether we are threatened or not. Sometimes, if we let go, wonderful surprises surface. Take advantage of those moments when your spouse is entranced for hours in front of the computer. It's an opportunity to strike out on your own—remembering all the while there are other activities to be shared with your spouse that you both enjoy. Computer addicts may be an extension of their computer, but you don't have to become an extension of your spouse.

Even though I had discovered a newfound freedom, I didn't take complete advantage of the situation. I didn't totally ignore my loved ones and it wasn't as if they entirely ignored me. I would occasionally meander by the room to see if they were still breathing (they all had a tendency to hyperventilate over some type of software recently purchased or resolving some mysterious happening).

Sometimes, they would call me into the room to share a new-fangled dooby bob and explain in great length its reason for being or doing whatever. At times, all three would encourage me to join in and learn what they discovered. They had unlimited time and patience to teach me anything I wanted to know about the computer, monitor, printer, or about things I couldn't see, like disk drives, megabytes, modems. I told them smugly, "I'm visual, I'm a designer; I like to type on a typewriter. Forget it." I resisted most of the time.

However, there were times when I felt I should learn a little something about computers now that I freelanced for a computer magazine and the world of telecommunications seemed to be passing me by. The ATM at my local bank seemed to glow as I walked by on my way to the friendly teller. Everywhere I turned, there seemed to be some type of machine to communicate with me.

astounding and I was equally amazed with their thinking process. It was definitely incredible. I was impressed and they knew it. All those years of nurturing paid off, I thought.

Of course, I took credit for their performance. It took no time at all to convince myself that they performed so well because of all the art projects I gave them to foster eye-hand coordination as they grew up.

Then doubt seeped into my mind. Could it be the result of early mornings before school at the local Seven/Eleven store playing video games when they told me they wanted to get to school early to play on the playground? Or the practice they got when their father and uncles would go to the "store" after a family gathering to purchase some urgent item and return with eyes glazed for hours afterwards? Or was their sureness of hand and intellectual quickness a result of years of exposure to the video games everywhere they turned?

I started to realize there are mindless, blow-them-up games, but there are also wonderful games to challenge a young person's mind and eye-hand coordination. Okay, so the games stayed—but so did my educational software.

Rule No. 8

When your family members agree too quickly to your demands, rules or commandments, beware.

The word "trust" should not be in your vocabulary when a computer shares your home. Unfortunately, when it comes right down to it, you might as well toss the word right out the window. You will come to comprehend that your dear ones will say and do anything to shut you up.

Your first clue is how quickly they agree with you. Your misgivings will come true. They want time with that computer, they won't let go of that computer and they will, without a doubt, have no guilt when they mislead you in thinking you will get what you ask for. Watch out because they're ruthless when it comes to their idol, their sunshine, their hero.

Rule No. 9

Don't assume something is detrimental to your child unless you can make a judgement from past experiences or until you have experienced what they have undergone.

Taking for granted that you know something will affect your child in a negative manner—without investigating the threat—can be detrimental to your child's mental or physical growth. Check it out. You may find that you are wrong in your assumptions. They're fearless and crave new experiences. We tend to play it safe. There is a happy medium and you may learn something astounding.

I was raised in an era when typewriters were exclusively used in the business world and xeroxes were beginning to edge out ditto machines. My long and tedious training in shorthand was put to short use when the dictating machine became the new kid on the block. I didn't feel threatened with the new way of doing things, but I did resist the new IBM Selectric Typewriter, the one with the ball that would spin as you typed. I loved my old IBM typewriter that seemed to be an extension of my hands, my arms, my whole being. I let my assistant have the new typewriter the company had bought for me.

No, I wasn't threatened, I just liked my old buddy better. As for the dictating machine, no thanks. The men I worked with preferred to dictate to me while I typed their letters as they spoke. We were a fast and accurate pair, my machine and me. I placed the new Selectric in the corner of my office and refused to let them sell my old one back to IBM. Instead I bought it from the company to assure myself that I would always have my dear friend near me. Years later, after abandoning my career to raise a family, I used my old typewriter for every typing chore possible.

When the computer entered into my life and our home, and after witnessing what it was capable of doing, I still couldn't imagine outputting a business or personal document using a computer. My trusted friend was still preferable.

What a hassle the computer seemed to me. With a typewriter, you just stick a piece of paper in it and start typing. My speed and accuracy were high and I could crank out something much faster than my husband could on his computer. Plus the type quality and look was more professional than a computer-generated document. "Forget the idea of switching," I told my husband. "I won't abandon my friend and I'm not threatened."

Unfortunately, I found myself in a position of having to write a paper soon after I declared my loyalty to my typewriter. I had done the necessary research and had all my facts in front of me to type my paper. My deadline was very close, too close for comfort. I rolled a piece of paper into my old and dear friend, mama IBM. My heart raced when nothing happened when I hit the first few keys. How could she fail me now? She had never broken down, never. Other than a new roller and an occasional cleaning, she was happy and healthy. The repair shop said it would be a week before I would get her back. That was past my deadline. My husband suggested the C-O-M-P-U-T-E-R! "No," I moaned. "I just can't." I needed my IBM, not that weird thing in the other room.

I tried to rent a typewriter. Too much money. I tried to borrow one. No one had an electric one. Meanwhile, precious time was ticking away madly. Finally, with the greatest of reluctance and resistance, I broke down and decided the computer was my only solution. My husband was full of ridiculous joy over my situation because I was finally where he wanted me to be: on the computer, ready for my first lesson.

I barked at him when he started in with his lengthy explanation of how to get where I should be to type this thing, how to type it, correct it, spell check it, save it, print it and then get out of where I was. My eyes glazed over as usual and I had an almost total loss of hearing. My body was someplace else. He was very patient and kind. I was irritable and spoke to him in short, curt and conde-scending sentences.

Nothing I said phased him. Didn't he get it? I absolutely hated being forced into this situation and he took no pity on me.

I knew he would soon leave for work and I would be left with a vague memory of what he told me. In desperation, I wrote down the fewest possible and most basic of commands. I put the phone by the computer and told him I would call if I got stuck. I typed like the wind but had a million mistakes. The keys on the keyboard were different than my old keyboard. Where was my correct-o tape? (The delete key was too easy and simple.) Arrows up and arrows down, page down and page up, arrows to the left and right. Where were my tabs? How could I indent? This seemed to such a stupid, time-consuming machine. I just wanted my typewriter back, now!

Somehow, I managed to get the paper printed, corrected, printed and corrected again to perfection. The type quality was still questionable, but I had finished in record time. I'd die first before I would admit that to anyone, especially my husband. That evening he praised me that I had handled my computer trauma well and was happily surprised that I managed to do everything by myself. He thought my new career in computers was just beginning.

As far as I was concerned, there was no career in computers, not as long as my mama IBM was still healthy. And the "A" on the paper that I received had absolutely nothing to do with the computer printout.

Rule No. 10

Plan to give up the old way of doing things and force yourself to accept new technology. You will be left in the dust, coughing and spitting, if you don't.

The more you fight change, the harder it will be for you to learn. Children have an incredible craving for knowledge and are not afraid of trying new things. If you try to become childlike, learning will become magical. Putting yourself in a position of "having" to learn rather than "wanting" to learn places you at a disadvantage. It makes learning harder. If you choose to gain knowledge voluntarily, it will not be a struggle and you will learn faster.

Rule No. 11

Being grumpy and resistant to any help on the computer will only be met with kind, patient and gentle assistance. They know, without a doubt, you will come to accept their way of thinking.

At first, you will firmly believe that if you are obvious in your disgust for the computer and its inner workings, your point will come across loud and clear. Your squawking, however, will fall on deaf ears. They are obnoxiously tolerant and enduring. You are the one who will suffer. They are like patient parents with the all-knowing wisdom that you will someday pass through your difficult teen years and blossom into a full-fledged, mature adult. Their motivation will be stronger than yours. You will end up banging your head against the wall in frustration if you resist.

Rule No. 12

Swallow your pride. Acknowledge that the computer will save you time, money and frustration.

It wouldn't hurt to say thanks to those gentle members of your family for helping you out in a time of crisis. After all, they weren't smug at all, at least *you* detected no such attitude. Sometimes it's hard to admit a new way works better than an old way. Swallow hard and say "thanks."

As the years skipped along, I began to notice how the computer had deeply changed the course of my older son's life. As a young child he had an intense interest in art. In fact, I sometimes think he came out of the womb clutching a pencil and drawing paper. I encouraged his interest and he continued to reflect an amazing aptitude for art. I was also pleased that we both shared the same interest. A career in art would be a dream come true.

Then the computer arrived in our home—and at his junior high. Now his new love, the computer, was competing neck and neck for his attention in art. Very little homework was getting done. What good grades he did get were in art, physical education and computers. How could a kid get Ds and Fs in his core classes and receive "a pleasure to have in class" under citizenship in those same classes?

He was so intelligent, if not gifted. I constantly asked myself, "Where did we go wrong?"

He was either programming or drawing. Any attempt on my part to change his behavior was useless. He heard the beat of a different drummer. I was convinced he graduated from high school simply because his teachers loved his creativity and pleasant personality.

I remember sitting in the football stadium graduation day. Grandma and Grandpa sat proudly with tears in their eyes as they saw their first-born grandson about to receive his diploma. My husband and I sat with our fingers crossed, exchanging glances, knowing what the other was thinking. He probably swiped the cap and gown and paid someone to call out his name so he could pick up his diploma. We didn't believe he made it until he went the next day to pick up his real diploma. We were in shock. So was he.

It was at this point that his interest in computers took over his love of art. He found a job at a software store. At first, it was exciting for him to be surrounded by every type of software imaginable. He learned the ins and outs of many programs and his customers loved him. However, it soon became boring, answering the same questions over and over again.

This boredom inspired him to start a computer consulting business of his own at the ripe age of 19. This may sound wonderful after what we experienced from his high school years. After all, he has direction, commitment and goals now.

Well, life is never simple. Earlier I complained that I had lost control of my home. Now the garage was confiscated for his business. Well, half a garage. He said needed an office to work out of and his bedroom was already full of equipment and the computer room was brimming full with his paperwork, disks, stereo equipment and other unrecognizable pieces of equipment.

Did I have a choice? I know better now than to think I did. Whenever I wasn't looking, he would swipe a shelf, a corner, a cranny or a nook. There had to be a limit! I howled to myself. I couldn't figure out for the life of me why I wasn't screaming bloody murder. In the back of my mind, there was always this nagging thought that if I squelched his creativity, his entrepreneurship, his risk-taking, I would be responsible for his business failing. I didn't want to take the chance and find out if I was right. If he needs the whole garage, so be it. I set a new limitation. Just stay out of my bedroom. That would be my new boundary line, I decided.

Rule No. 13

Brace yourself. You will soon come to the realization that you have very little control over your child's destiny. Especially, when a computer is competing for their attention.

One of the hardest ideas for parents to comprehend is, as their children grow older, they have less and less control over what their children do or say. This is nature's law and as it should be. You should plan on not fighting Mother Nature and her calling. It's easy when they're young to guide them, participate in their activities and share special moments with them. Appreciate and relish this time. As they enter junior high and high school, the "push away" begins. You know less and less about what they do and where they're going or what they are thinking.

Oh, you may think you know, but you don't know at all. They only tell you what they want you to know.

When you first set eyes on your precious newborn, you will have hopes and dreams for them. But just remember, these are *your* hopes and dreams, not theirs. Let go and flow with their interests. You may be happily surprised with their choices. In the beginning, I was disappointed with my son's switch in careers because computers seemed so left-brained and that was foreign to me. I do believe, now, that the way he uses computers is definitely right-brained. He must be creative to do what he does with computers.

Rule No. 14

Put your foot down, hard, when it comes to your space and time. Otherwise, your computer-obsessed family members will take advantage of your good nature and you will be considered an enabler of their inappropriate actions.

It's one thing to encourage creativity—totally another thing to give up certain rights and freedoms that should be obvious to most normal co-residents of a home. Stick to your guns, because if you give an inch, they will take a yard. Guard every nook and cranny of your home. I know from experience that they are relentless in their pursuit of space. Your home will become a paper mill and they will act as if it's someone else's mess when you complain.

If you allow them to permeate your home gradually, you are enabling their behavior. Believe me, their psyche won't be harmed. They will survive your ranting and raving. Whether they listen to you is another matter, but you should at least continue your battle against their invasion at any cost.

RULES TO LIVE BY: WIDOWHOOD SURVIVAL

Rule No. 1

If you are outnumbered in your home, you will lose every battle associated with a computer.

Rule No. 2

The computer will become a permanent resident of your home. Believe the certainty of this law.

Rule No. 3

If you think your home really belongs to you when the computer occupies a spot in it, you have a huge illusion to overcome.

Rule No. 4

You will feel threatened in the beginning when the computer enters your home and you will also deny this emotion vehemently. Cave in now and greet it with open, loving arms.

Rule No. 5

Realize from the very onset that your dear loved ones know the eventual outcome of your overt or covert resistance long before you do. They have developed a sixth sense.

Rule No. 6

Don't overlook a glaring advantage in your widowhood state of being that might be staring you right in the face.

Rule No. 7

Don't pass up the opportunity to learn something, anything, from your computer nerds. Basic information can be valuable to you in the future.

Rule No. 8

When your family members agree too quickly to your demands, rule or commandments, suspect something immediately.

Rule No. 9

Don't assume something is detrimental to your child unless you can make a judgement from past experiences or until you have experienced what they have undergone.

Rule No. 10

Plan to give up the old way of doing things and force yourself to accept new technology. You will be left in the dust, coughing and spitting, if you don't.

Rule No. 11

Being grumpy and resistant to any help on the computer will only be met with kind, patient and gentle assistance. They know, without a doubt, that you will come to accept their way of thinking.

Rule No. 12

Swallow your pride and acknowledge that the computer saved you time, money and frustration.

Rule No. 13

Brace yourself. You will soon come to the realization that you have very little control over your child's destiny. Especially when a computer is competing for their attention.

Rule No. 14

Put your foot down, hard, when it comes to your space and time. Otherwise, they will take advantage of your good nature and you will be considered an enabler of their inappropriate actions.

I have listed above the rules that I now live by in order to survive living in a home with three computer nerds. These are rules that you should take seriously and imbed in your mind. You may resist in the beginning, as I did, but I can guarantee that you will come around to my way of thinking eventually. Save yourself from frustration, heartache and headaches. They will win, whether you are outnumbered or not, by their sheer persistence and patience. They know the computer will become a permanent fixture in your home even though you have other thoughts or devious plans to rid yourself of the unsightly mess.

Let go of your anxiety and resistance. Come around now to the conclusion that every part of your home is under attack. Strive to save the dearest parts. Save your rage and strength for the most important items on your list. They may listen from time to time.

Fighting advancements in technology and then denying those true feelings is like swimming upstream or going against the grain. Join the crowd and accept rather than feel threatened about computers. The sooner you come around the quicker you will learn. Everyone else knows you will eventually break down. The only one that doesn't is you.

Jump in and look for advantages to widowhood. Not only should you learn something new at every opportunity from your knowledgeable group but you should also strike out on your own. Laying around moaning about how tough it is being a computer widow is acting like a martyr. Stop acting like a victim. Peel off your suffering attitude and discover things that you can do on you own. If you don't understand their fetish with the computer and have no plans to join them, then find other things to do. Remember, don't be an extension of their beings.

While you are off exploring new positive avenues in your life, keep both eyes on your beloved group. All those promises to change and quick verbal agreements should be examined closely. Your nerds are definitely up to some type of mischief. Be suspicious at all times. Don't forget, too, their patience and sixth sense of knowing what you will do long before you know.

Right from the beginning, save yourself a little pride by acknowledging that you can learn something from your children, spouse and friends. Admit, too, that the computer can actually help you in a crisis, not to mention on a frequent basis.

I know that it's hard to believe that you have very little control over your life and even less over your children's lives when it comes to computers. They come, you guide, you love, you nurture, you teach, you set an exemplary example of how to live as a human being, and then they do what they want regardless. You can fuss and carry on but you can only control so much. We all have our destinies.

If I had only known ten years ago when the computer first arrived on our doorstep that I would ultimately approve of and adopt a positive attitude toward this addition to our family, it would have saved me years of anguish. I still have no great desire to spend the hours they do with the computer. It doesn't make my heart beat fast with joy, as does a good art project, or a beautiful painting, or a well-designed brochure, but at least I'm not as threatened as I was and I can approach it without trepidation.

It has not touched my life as dramatically as my family's lives. My husband uses it extensively for his business and our personal documentation. It's now my older son's livelihood. And as for my younger son, he uses it for school projects and games (we've given him the title "King of Games").

The future of the computer in our home is very bright. It will always have a shining spot in our home. As much as I fought, scratched and clawed for the demise of this thing, I'm very glad I lost the battle.

The computer has enhanced our lives tremendously and I wouldn't change a thing. I'm just glad that I had formidable opponents to fend off my constant, aggressively resistant moves.

"You've got to be kidding! This is terrible!"

CHAPTER 3

Writings of Computer Widow/Widower's Contest Winners

We knew they were out there—the silent, suffering minority. We knew of their pain and solitude, and were determined to bring their plight out into the open.

In the summer of 1989, we announced an all-out search for the longest-suffering, most put-upon, most thoroughly disgusted computer widows and widowers in our local area, requesting their tales of woe and cartoons. And they heard our call and responded with floods of stories, poems, cartoons and bitter, irate testimonies.

It broke our hearts to hear of their plight, these blitzed and bewildered by-products of the Age of Technology, these forgotten and disregarded spouses. There personal stories were harrowing—some had spouses who only emerged from the computer room to grab some sort of packaged snack food or diet soda from the kitchen. They were ignored, rejected and dejected.

It was difficult to decide, but we finally chose three winners: Stephanie Atlas, author of "Birth of a Computer Widow"; Maxine Edwards, author of "Computer Widow (the Poem)"; and Gary Middeke, who drew the winning cartoon, "Testimony of a Computer Widow." We congratulate and thank these articulate and expressive, and now publically acknowledged, computer widows and widower. We hope you will enjoy their offerings.

BIRTH OF A COMPUTER WIDOW
By Stephanie Atlas

In a little room at the top of the stairs, dark except for a soft green glow that emanates from a screen, my husband whirs and taps his fingers away. This goes on for days at a time.

"At least he doesn't go out with the guys for beer and come home burping," said my mother one evening on the phone.

"Burping would be great," I said. "All I get is beeping."

"You really should try to join in his activities," was my mother's advice. This is a woman who carpeted her home with Astroturf and spoke to my father in a huddle during football season. But it was worth a try.

That afternoon, I went to a custom nightgown store and ordered one to be made up. At night I stood in front of a mirror in a long pink negligee with a silkscreened keyboard across my chest. The "shift" key had been strategically placed.

"Well, goodnight," I said seductively while passing by his open door.

"Oh yeah," he said not looking up from his monitor. "Sleep well." He frowned and started to shuffle some disks around.

"Problems?" I asked sympathetically.

"Just a little trouble with my hard drive," he said.

"I know, dear. The news said the traffic was horrendous this afternoon."

He looked up slightly bewildered. "You know, pink really isn't your color." I stood riveted to my spot, refusing to be deleted.

"I really made a mistake with this compatible," he said.

"That's not true," I said, growing concerned. "We love the same movies and our values are very similar."

"What are you jabbering on about, Stephanie?" he asked, growing irritated. The phone rang, and when he picked it up he was immediately involved in conversation. I overheard something about a nibble and wisely decided to bring him up some hot cocoa and cookies.

Upon returning, I noticed he was down on his hands and knees behind the desk.

"What are you doing?" I asked.

"Just looking for the mouse."

"Oh my God!" I screamed, dropping the cookies on the floor and heading for the nearest chair. "Call somebody quick!"

"No, this is a Genius Mouse," he said calmly.

"I just hope it doesn't outsmart Terminex," I said, quivering.

When the doctor informed me that my tiredness and inability to hold down food was due to my recent pregnancy, I shot him a look.

"That's impossible," I said, explaining my situation.

"We did have that power failure about a month ago," he reminded me.

"Oh yes," I smiled fondly at the memory. It's the same smile I use when I remember the time I stubbed my toe while bowling.

When I raced home, I found my husband had just turned on his printer and was eating a hot dog.

"Can we go somewhere quiet to talk?" I asked. "I have a little surprise for you."

He scratched his head. "In a minute; I just noticed that I lost a byte."

I looked down at his half-eaten hot dog. "Well, certainly you aren't accusing me," I said. "I just got here. Maybe it was that mouse. But this is no time to talk about food. We're going to have a baby."

I watched as he turned a shade of green that rivaled his monitor. As his breath quickened, a shaky hand reached for the keyboard, and without hesitating, he firmly struck the "Escape" key.

"Oh no you don't," I said. "Not this time, buddy." After studying the keyboard myself the other day, I knew exactly where it was. To his great shock and surprise, I reached over his shoulder and with a quick flick of my wrist, I hit the "home" key.

Several months later, I walked in on my husband as he triumphantly held up a long printout.

"I did it!" he beamed.

"What did you do?" I inquired.

"These are the spreadsheets that show what the baby's feeding schedule will be," he said proudly.

I was truly touched. "So, you have been thinking about this baby!"

"Quite a bit," he said. "If it's a boy, what do you think about the name MacArthur? Or maybe MacMartin?"

"Those are nice," I said politely, not wanting to dampen his enthusiasm. "What would you like for dinner?"

"How about MacDonald's?" he said with a grin. "Oh, I almost forgot; I have something for you."

"You do?" I said smiling as I watched him pull a package from the desk drawer.

As I eagerly tore at the wrapper, I found a blue T-shirt in a large size that had printing on the front in large black letters.

It said "A Chip off the Old Clone," and an arrow pointed down to where my stomach would be.

"You really shouldn't have," I said.

"It's okay; I had a little money left from the laptop."

"Laptop?" I asked, thinking how much I despised those yappy little dogs. I hoped he hadn't bought a poodle.

"Yes, it's a portable computer I can bring with us to the hospital," he said. "For the delivery room. I worked out a program to time your contractions and pinpoint exactly when the baby will come."

When I left the room, I heard him phoning his good friend DOS. I couldn't help but overhear when I passed by the door.

"I don't know DOS, I've got to get rid of this tired, old, beat-up floppy. Got any takers?"

I looked down at myself. It's true, I hadn't exercised lately, and you could call me a little flabby, but floppy was taking it too far. Of course, it could be these old house slippers I keep wearing.

"Sure I might trade. What'ya wanna offer me?" he paused. "I might consider that. Dot matrix?"

I mentally racked my brain trying to remember who this could be. I don't even know any Dorothys, let alone Dots. When I could take it no more, I ran crying into his office and flopped down on the couch.

"Gotta go, DOS. Problems." He hung up. It took four hours for him to comfort me and a promise that he would remove the terminal he had recently installed in the headboard of our king size bed.

When it came time for our baby shower, my husband stayed locked away in the room for hours. One guest who happened to pass by the room looking for the bathroom came running to me, breathless.

"Something's going on in there," she said, imitating the noises she had heard. She lowered her voice. "Something sinister."

"It's just my husband with his Apple," I said confidently.

"Oh no," she said shaking her head, "there's something much more than fruit in there, honey!"

After everyone left, I managed to coax him downstairs to see all the gifts. Cribs, strollers and bibs were strewn everywhere. "Wasn't everyone thoughtful?" I asked.

"We didn't even get the essentials," he said dismayed. "Where's the pacifier shaped like an adaptor? And how about "Baby's First Modem?"

"But we got this adorable stuffed frog named Kermit," I said, holding up the green figure.

"Kermit?" he asked, and I watched his ears perk up.

When the day finally came, I stood in the doorway, watching my husband.

"It's time," I said.

"Time?" he repeated, busily moving his fingers.

I took a deep breath. "Time for retrieving a file. Baby 4.0."

"Look, Stephanie, I think it's really cute that you're trying to learn the lingo, but ..." He looked up at me. I nodded. Turning off his computer, he ran out the door, but not before grabbing his laptop. We had a hard drive on the way to the hospital. First we ran out of gas and then we had to stop at a store that had a sale on laser printers.

"Slow down," I demanded, as we approached a yellow light.

"Bad command," he said as we zoomed through.

All through labor my husband was extremely supportive. He held my hand, mopped my brow and kept whispering encouragingly into my ear, "Okay, honey. Get ready, one, two, three. It's almost time to RAM."

"That's push, sir," said one of the nurses. "It's almost time to push." He gave her a dirty look. "I knew that."

At one point, he looked from me to his monitor and back again.

"You know, your contractions are coming a lot quicker than the computer says they should."

"Oh really," I said, trying not to huff. "Well, you can tell your computer . . ."

But I was seized with another contraction that the computer said didn't exist.

When the doctor finally held up our 7-pound baby girl and asked what her name would be, I looked at my husband to see his reaction.

"That's okay," he said. "I came fully prepared. Her name is Irene Bernadette." He pulled out a bracelet from his pocket.

I smiled at him to show I approved of the beautiful name. Our last name was Martin and it all fit perfectly. As he hooked the little bracelet on our new daughter, he handed her to me. "Just thought I would have her initials engraved," he said.

I looked down at the silverplated links around her tiny wrist and read the initials aloud with horror: "I.B.M."

"Sedative," I groaned and lapsed into unconsciousness.

COMPUTER WIDOW POEM
By Maxine Edwards

After 40 years with the love of my life,
I now feel like a neglected wife.
A computer has come to our house—
Good heavens, there's even a mouse.
Now, my honey kisses me good night;
It's not as if we really fight.
He disappears in the night gloom,
To be alone in the PC room.

I awake, the clock says four,
Open is the bedroom door.
Empty is his side of the bed,
Does he have the instructions read?
Daytime chores he does in a flurry,
Rushes to the computer, eyes blurry.
He's into graphs, and menu screens,
Printing changes from grey to green.
Seems our marriage has gone to pot,
I'm determined, this must stop.

While he is out, I rush to the machine
First I dust it nice and clean.
Plug it in, and it talks to me,
"I was used at 4:03."
I push a key and it yells at me,
"Bad command, don't you see?"

The manual says I can draw & paint,
Should I do a masterpiece landscape?
Whoa—this is getting to be fun,
Make stick figures, see them run!

Our marriage has been saved you see,
And the perfect idea just came to me.
We now have two PCs snuggled close.
It's where we meet for coffee and toast.
Our conversations had been getting worse,
This is why I started writing this verse.
Marital problem solved in PC time.
I put "I love you" on his PC line.

WINNING CARTOON
By Gary L. Middeke

Testimony of a Computer Widow
By Gary L. Middeke

"...My rendition of 'mental cruelty?' He named our daughter 'UNIX' and our son 'Chip.' He refers to the baby as 'a laptop.' Anything beyond our front yard is 'public domain.' We don't buy shoes – we 're-boot.' If I get mad at the children, he says I'm 'mother-bored.' In short, Your Honor – I wanna re-format my marital status!"

GRETA LONGWYND'S
LINGERING, LONGING LAPTOP OF

LOVE

CHAPTER 4

The Lingering, Longing
Laptop of Love
By Greta Longwynd

The sun was a blazing crimson orb as it rose majestically between the twin peaks of Mount Betsy and Mount Moo. Clarissa Carmichael stood at the cusp of the valley gazing upward, milk pail in hand, breathing deeply the fragrant aroma of morning. Bathed in the sun's ruddy glow, she was as much a part of the ranch as the dewy grass and the pungent fertilizer surrounding her.

Carmichael Cattle Ranch lay to the east of Myrtletown, a booming, budding Western metropolis. Clarissa had been born there, raised by her father after the untimely and tragic death of her mother (who slipped on a cow pie and fell face first into a branding iron), many years before. Clarissa had never felt cheated or deprived; she and her father were the world to each other. Bud Carmichael had raised his daughter as almost an equal, letting her speak her mind and cavort about in knickers.

Some said Clarissa Carmichael was too willful and stubborn for her own good, and that Bud had raised an unmarriageable and incorrigible daughter. But Bud respected her keen mind, and had taught her everything he knew about the ranch. As he grew older, greyer, feebler, fatter and a little lazier he came to rely on his daughter for running most of the business of the ranch.

On this particular morning, as Clarissa stood basking barefoot in the mud, her thoughts were on her beloved ranch. Her father's 60th birthday was approaching, and Clarissa knew that at last her father would be turning the deed to the ranch officially over to her. At 19, and being a woman, she knew that others thought her a strange old maid to revel in the workings of an admittedly untidy cattle ranch. "Let them scoff!" she thought, tossing her long auburn hair. The fragrant trees, the majestic cattle, the flies, were all as much a part of her as her milky white skin and fiery temper.

With a deep breath, followed by a delicate gag, she surveyed her land once again and turned back toward the house. And in the hidden shadows of a dark oak nearby, Vick Sloan deeply inhaled his unfiltered Camel cigarette and watched her leave. He pulled the cigarette from his lips and slowly blew smoke through his nose. His lips curled into a sinister smile as he watched the unsuspecting young firebrand. Vick Sloan had long coveted both Carmichael Cattle Ranch and Clarissa Carmichael. Soon, he chuckled to himself, both would be his.

Clarissa sensed trouble as soon as she entered the dining room. Her father sat at the head of the table clutching a piece of paper, his face ashen, his prunes untouched before him. He looked up, swallowed painfully and motioned for Clarissa to come sit beside him.

"Father, what's wrong? It isn't gas, is it? Shall I prepare an antacid?

"No, no child. Just sit here next to me." Bud gazed into his daughter's face, which so painfully reminded him of the face of his beloved wife Corinna—before the accident, of course.

"I have something to tell you ..." he faltered, took a sip of juice and turned to face his daughter. "The ranch is no longer mine."

"Oh, father, this is the happiest day of my life. You're finally turning Carmichael Cattle Ranch over to me. I have so many ideas, you'll be so proud of me—"

"Stop! No, you don't understand." Bud shifted his mammoth girth to turn away from Clarissa. "I've always dreamed of turning the ranch over to you. I never wished for a boy to carry on my name, at least, not after you were 16 or 17, but ..."

Exasperated, Clarissa took her father by the shoulders and shook him. "What have you done?"

"I've lost the ranch."

Clarissa sat back, stunned. "What? How?"

"A few days ago. It was a poker game. Three-card monte, deuces and jokers wild. It was down to me and Vick the Banker, $50,000 versus the ranch. I thought I could read his face, I thought he must have three of a kind, but I didn't listen to myself. No, I went with the odds and drew..."

"I don't want to hear this. I can't believe this. Father, do you know what you've done? You've lost our home, our livelihood, to the most hateful and ugly man in Myrtletown."

Bud looked up with tears in his eyes. "Vick has offered to be merciful. He'll let us stay on here, collect a salary, but only if..."

"If what?" Clarissa asked suspiciously.

Bud smiled hopefully. "Vick's not such a bad guy, huh? He makes a good living. Sure, he's got that overbite and that glandular problem, and sure he's a little moody, but you could do a lot worse."

Clarissa's eyes widened in horror. "You can't be serious."

"Sweetie, face it. Your marriage prospects were dim, anyway."

"How can you say that? What about my milky white skin and shining auburn hair?"

"Well, yes, of course, but dear you're a daunting prospect, always challenging the boys to bull-wrestling contests. Maybe I've treated you too much like a son. Maybe Vick and I are doing you a favor here." Bud's face brightened. "Yeah, maybe marriage to Vick will bring out the sweet domestic servility you—"

"Oh, shut up, Father."

There was silence for a few moments. Finally Bud spoke softly. "Clarissa, if you don't marry Vick he'll sell the land to condo developers, he'll sell the cattle to the leather accessory company, and I'll lose my home."

Clarissa sighed and clenched her hands. "I guess I haven't much choice." She brightened a little. "But I'll still run the ranch; not much will change; right, Father?"

Bud's smile wavered a little. "Well, dear, there's more. Vick has decided to bring in a computer consultant to re-vamp the ranch."

"A computer on a ranch? You're not serious. Now that's the most ridiculous thing I've ever heard. How much more will be asked of me? How much more must I take? First I must give my body to a foul-smelling, chain smoking banker, and then my mind to a heartless mechanical box." With an anguished cry, Clarissa flew from the room, leaving Bud alone, a broken man eating prunes.

* * * * * * * * * * * *

Rex Holcroft strode confidently through the manure-peppered field, carefully balancing his magnesium-coated '386 laptop. He was a proud man, an independent consultant under contract to Vick Sloan to develop expediency programs for Carmichael Ranch. It would be a quick job, done well and thoroughly, and like most of his jobs, he would not get emotionally involved. Rex solved problems, and he did it his way, leaving when he felt the time was right.

Some called him arrogant, blunt, hard and uncaring. He had no problem with that. He'd been hurt too much to ever let himself care again. He'd lost too much of himself networking and programming, developing systems for others who took his programs and used them, misused them, never even reading the documentation, let alone utilizing the full capabilities of the software. He was through with all that. He was a hardened programmer there to perform a function; never again would he get emotionally involved. Ever.

Vick Sloan paced the living room of the ranch house, stopping every so often to finger one of the delicate antique cow sculptures that decorated the room. Bud sat in an overstuffed armchair, his lifeless gaze and lumpy form a pathetic sight. Clarissa sat straight up on a hard chair, glaring at Vick and following his every move.

"I've called you both here this evening to discuss my plans for my ranch."

"Your ranch!" Clarissa spat indignantly. "The deed may be in your name, but never will this land or this livestock be yours!"

"Quiet, you conceited, cow-loving twit." Vick's nostrils flared. "There's going to be some changes around here, starting with you. You will be seen and not heard. You will keep your mouth shut, and you will do exactly as I say."

"Never!"

"If you don't cooperate, he'll—" Vick gestured toward Bud— "be put out to pasture."

Bud burped.

Clarissa's hand flew to her mouth in horror. She sat back quietly in her chair.

Vick sneered. "Now that's more like it. First of all, I've hired Rex Holcroft, computer consultant, to re-vamp the ranch to *my* specifications. We'll computerize the cow branding process; we'll keep a database of cows' health, age, everything! I'll control it all!" Vick clasped his hands together with glee. "I'll have productivity reports on all the employees; we'll fire half and the computers will do the rest! And soon I'll take over more and more of Myrtletown."

Clarisssa stood and clenched her fists with anger. "Fire my staff? Never! Never will a plastic-coated bucket of bolts take the place of my cowhands. Sure, they're a little slow, and yes, they work in manure fields, but they have hearts of gold and loyalty that no overpriced electronic calculator will ever have."

As Clarissa spoke, Rex Holcroft stood immobile and unseen in the shadows of the doorway of the living room. He stood, unable to move and breathe, so transfixed was he by the sight of the passionate and voluptuous vixen who spoke with such ringing passion of the value of human loyalty. The setting sun cast amber shadows over her auburn hair, causing a rosy halo to shine over her head. In that instant, Rex knew that he was completely and totally in love with the auburn-haired stranger.

So captivated was he by the vision of loveliness before him that he didn't notice Vick's eyes upon him.

"Well, well, Mr. Holcroft. You've finally arrived." Vick's eyes lit up.

Startled by the guttural tones of the banker's voice after the dulcet sweetness of Clarissa's speech, Rex turned, tripped and dropped the '386 laptop.

Clarissa screamed, Bud almost got out of his chair and Vick's eyes narrowed with fury.

"You fool!" Vick spat. "Don't ruin my plans before we even have a chance to begin.

Rex bent to pick up the machine. "Don't worry. The hard magnesium cover case, coupled with the internally soldered head pins, render this baby indestructible."

Clarissa knelt beside Rex as he closed the open laptop lid. Gently, she reached out to dust off a scrap of manure from the keyboard. At the same time, Rex's hand moved to wipe the same lone fertilizer chunk, and in an instant their hands met. Clarissa's modest downcast eyes looked up and met his, and she caught her breath, caught by the keenly intelligent gaze of the computer man.

"I ... I hope it isn't damaged, sir."

Rex coughed slightly and pushed his bifocals further up his nose bridge. "Why, no, it's fine and ..." his words trailed off in a hopeless, meaningless confusion as his impassioned gaze sought the eyes and face of his five-foot-two, auburn-haired destiny.

"Just pick the damn thing up and get over here," Vick spat with annoyance. "I'm not paying you by the hour to ogle my fiance."

At that instant, the bottom dropped out of Rex's world. His mouth flew open and he felt a crimson flush spread across his admittedly pale face. His gaze flew back to Clarissa, his expression one of pained disbelief, imploring her to say it wasn't so, that it was all a cruel cosmic joke, that all meaning hadn't just been stripped from his life, that the delicate pastry-fed flower before him wasn't soon to be the wanton plaything of the evil snake who paid his salary.

Clarissa bit her lip and avoided his gaze. She, too had been struck by Cupid's thunderbolt of destiny and was decidedly miffed that his timing was so off. With a nervous, timid smile at Rex she rose to her feet, turned and gave Vick a black look and gracefully sat on the ottoman beside her father.

Rex shook his head and tried to get a grip on the events at hand. He stood up, dusted himself off and gently brought the laptop over to the table where Vick stood.

Vick snorted disgustedly (and, Clarissa thought, disgustingly). "Rex Holcroft, computer consultant, meet Bud Carmichael, esteemed business whiz and, fortunately, *former* owner of this ranch." Bud sat dozing in the armchair, delicately snoring. Clarissa reached up and gave him a sharp elbow in the ribs. Bud woke with a jolt, looked at Clarissa with sleepy confusion, then caught sight of Rex and Vick.

"Oh, hello there." He cleared his throat and propped himself up further in the chair, nervously smiling.

"And this," Vick said with a lascivious smile and a gleam lighting his eyes, "is my fiance, Clarissa Carmichael."

Clarissa tossed her long auburn hair, unfortunately whipping Bud in the face. "How do you do," she murmured as Bud stifled a yowl.

Rex was a computer consultant, a programmer, a man of numbers and figures and formulas and logic. Yet for the first time a figure was clouding his brain and his judgement, and that was the figure of one Clarissa Carmichael. "No," he thought. "I will not be taken in by this red-haired seductress. I'm a free man with only a laptop for a friend, coming and going when I please. Besides, she's marrying my boss."

His heart thus hardened, Rex nodded coldly toward Clarissa, then turned to listen to Vick.

"So you received my input and all the figures. What have you come up with?" Vick impatiently twisted his cowhide watch.

All business now after his brief foray into the turmoil of love at first sight, Rex crisply opened the laptop and began typing.

"A most interesting case study, Carmichael Cattle Ranch," Rex began. "The main profit problem as I see it is disorganization. Over 500 acres and 600 cattle, at various stages of growth, health, and hide. You've got the cow feed problems, the manure business on the side is sucking profits, the land upkeep, births, deaths, a staff that's doing god knows what behind your back ..."

Clarissa's nostrils flared with fury. "My men are trusted employees who would gladly give their lives for me, my cows, and my fertilizer. Sure it's hard work but I'd like to see that thing—" she gestured with annoyance at the computer—"try and keep up with everything."

Rex tried to ignore the way her nostrils delicately flared like pink shells along the shores of a sandy beach, and the way her breasts heaved with emotion, and—

"Well, answer me, dammit!"

"Clarissa!" Bud smiled sheepishly at Vick and Rex. "She's been a little on edge lately."

"Quite all right." Rex answered crisply, trying to suppress the flush he knew was spreading across his face. Taking a deep breath, he looked squarely at Clarissa. "I'll tell you how this *thing* will keep up with everything." Savoring the expectant silence in the room, he looked smugly at Vick, then Bud, then Clarissa.

"I've written, devised, documented and downloaded the ultimate in cattle-ranch-running software. Lady and gentlemen, I give you *CowBase*."

Rex punched in a few keys and turned the screen around. Clarissa and Bud strained to see, and Vick knelt with complete absorption. On the screen, a digital cow blinked on and off amid the image of the ranch while the words "*CowBase*, written by Rex

Holcroft, devised specifically for the cows, cattle and convenience of Vick Sloan and the Carmichael Cattle Ranch" ran across the screen.

"Incredible," Vick whispered reverently.

Clarissa stared at the screen with wonder and fear, wanting to touch it but daring not to. "What will it do, sir?" she asked timidly.

"Everything," Rex answered simply, pushing his glasses up his nose with pride. "It will keep track of, control, regulate and moderate every aspect of running this ranch. Your profits will increase to a degree inversely proportionate to the cattle ranch bell curve standard. You and your—" he swallowed distastefully— "husband will be able to control everything from the privacy of your own office."

"She won't have anything to do with any business," Vick responded impatiently. "She'll be too busy performing her pre-or-dained womanly functions."

Clarissa's eyes flashed with fury. "You pig," she whispered. Her rigid glance then fell upon Rex and the computer. For a moment her eyes softened, but she quickly hardened her heart and her stare. For a few fleeting seconds earlier, when their hands had meet above the scrap of manure, she had felt a yearning to be near him such as she had never felt before for someone who wasn't a cow. In that instant she had thought him her kindred spirit, a soulmate with eyes that reflected her own loneliness and pain. But here he was, suddenly the enemy, plotting with ingenious computer expertise the downfall of her beloved ranch. In league with disgusting and distasteful Vick Sloan no less, whom she would sooner murder than marry if Bud wasn't such a pathetic dependent drunken sot.

And that deceptively innocent computer, with pictures of friendly cows dancing across its screen. It too joined the ranks of heartless men and machines who strived to snatch her life's blood. The computer was, in fact the key to the downfall of the ranch.

Clarissa sighed, her frustration and fury giving way to heart-rending pain. With a strangled cry, she flew from the room.

Vick shrugged and turned back to the computer screen. With devious, evil delight he explored menus and help screens with frenetic glee.

Bud slowly rose from his chair, the stone weight of failure and regret heavy upon his already heavy frame. He moved himself over to the bar and poured a Scotch. It wasn't his first of the evening and would by no means be his last.

Rex stood by Vick, feeling oddly empty. Normally a client's delight in his superior, brilliant programming sent waves of pride coursing through his body. Now all that coursed through his body was nausea at the thought of the Carmichael family being torn apart by the greed of the chain smoking, pock marked, actually rather disgusting man who paid him enormous quantities of money. With a disheartened shrug, he bent to help Vick through the tutorial of his brilliant program.

Clarissa flew from the house in anguish. Disoriented, she stood on the porch for a moment breathing deeply of the pungent evening air. Calmer, she began walking barefoot through the fields, toward one of her favorite cattle pens. Outside in the fields with her feet unshod, breathing the rich fragrant cow smell which was so much a part of her, she felt saddened. For 19 years she had lived, breathed, ate, slept and smelled like this ranch. Maybe it wasn't operating at full profit, but what was money anyway? There was always enough for her and Bud to eat, and the staff made honest, good livings. The cows were peaceful, happy critters, and up until they were slaughtered, they were quite content.

Clarissa hoisted herself upon the wooden fence and sat gazing at the stars. A part of her felt that she couldn't remain here and watch her nice, old-fashioned ranch turn into an episode of "Star Trek." "*CowBase*," she whispered with anguished fear.

Then there was the matter of her impending marriage to Vick Sloan, a nauseating prospect to say the least. Could she in all sanity remain here married to a man with a severe overbite and glandular problem, who ran her beautiful ranch from a computer terminal in the living room? No, she couldn't—she wouldn't! If only it wasn't for—Bud.

She sighed. Her father would be a pathetic sight if taken from the ranch. Actually, he was a pathetic sight even now, and it was unthinkable even to speculate about Bud out of his element.

What other choice did she have? Stay here and fight a losing, humiliating battle against a computer; or stay here and give in to a bleak, meaningless computerized existence; or run away and live with the responsibility of her father's ruination. She sighed again, and rubbed her temples.

Then there was Rex, the cruelest plot twist the story of her life had yet taken. The tall (well, medium height), luminescently pale, bespeckled stranger whose keen intellect and brilliance shone through even the thick glass of his bifocals. The computer man who in an instant had seemed to represent everything abundantly human. How cruel fate was to let her glimpse unity with a soulmate, only to snatch away her hopes and dreams in the blink of an eye.

"Oh Rex!" she cried, opening her arms to the sky. "You corralled my heart and emblazoned it with the branding iron of your love, only to cast me away, a marked woman. I could have tolerated Vick if I hadn't met you, if I hadn't caught a whiff of the odor of true passion." Clarissa covered her face with her hands and sobbed.

And several yards away, Rex Holcroft stood in the shadows, entranced by the moonlit chit. Unable to bear her anguished cries, he threw caution to the wind and called out to her. "Hey!"

Startled, Clarissa whirled around, a difficult maneuver when one is sitting on a wooden fence above a cow pen. Delicately, gracefully, yet distressingly soundly, she fell to the muddy ground of the corral. With a dismayed yelp, Clarissa tried to unstick herself from the muddy earth.

Rex ran forward, quickly climbed the fence, and with an unfortunate lack of coordination soon joined Clarissa and the cows in the dirt.

Clarissa stopped pulling mud from her hair and gazed at Rex. "You! What do you want from me now? What are you doing here? I hate you, I tell you, I hate you for trying to take away my ranch."

Rex had trouble speaking, but after wiping the dirt from his mouth, he began. "Clarissa, I heard you talking to yourself, talking about me. Can it be true? Is it me you love and not Vick Sloan?"

"Oh, for heaven's sake, think about it! He's evil incarnate, vile, disgusting—and what are you doing helping him take away my ranch?"

"Take away the ranch? I was helping you all to *keep* the place. Vick sent me the figures, and it was obvious the place was going under when your father sold it to him."

"Vick Sloan never bought this ranch!" Clarissa cried. "He tricked my poor father during a poker game. He's had his devious mind set on owning Carmichael Cattle Ranch for as long as I can remember." Clarissa swallowed painfully. "And he's had his vile heart set on owning me ever since I hit puberty."

Rex stared at Clarissa, his hand thoughtfully rubbing his chin. "Vick said you'd been engaged for years, and that you've wanted this all along."

"Lies, lies, all lies!" Clarissa's voice was impassioned, her eyes pleading. "You must believe me! I've been running this place for years, not Bud. I know all the figures and we were doing fine—no great profits, but nowhere near going under. Vick is a heartless monster who wants to drain all the ranch's money into his devious plot to overtake all of Myrtletown. And he's using you and your computer to do it!"

Tears sprung from her eyes, mingling with the dirt on her face. Gently, Rex reached out to flick the hardened mud from her cheek. "I've been such a fool. I've been blind and greedy, caring only about my own career while that evil scoundrel has plotted your ruin."

Gazing into each others' dirt-encrusted faces, Clarissa and Rex were suddenly struck by overwhelming love and passion.

"Clarissa!" Rex moaned.

"Rex!" Clarissa whispered breathlessly, then flung herself into his arms, locking in a passionate embrace. And that tender moment of splendor in the mud sealed and consecrated their love for each other.

"But wait," Rex broke away. "There's one thing you don't understand. The computer is being used for evil by Vick, but it is a truly noble tool, which can help the ranch beyond your wildest dreams. *CowBase* is just the beginning of the ways my computer and I can make this ranch the best in the world."

Clarissa's eyes narrowed. "I don't want that heartless mechanical monster to take my peoples' jobs away, and to take me away from the land."

Rex laughed softly. "But you're so wrong. My computers will create *more* jobs, and together we'll train everyone to compute!"

"But what about Vick Sloan? He's threatened my father, he's threatened me, and he sort of *did* win the ranch in that poker game."

"I'll take care of Vick Sloan," Rex asserted. "In a court of law, Bud could be convicted of ignorance and stupidity, and maybe illegal gambling, but no one would sentence him to life without a ranch. Besides, I've accessed Sloan's personal business records, and what I know could put him away for life."

"Oh, Rex," Clarissa sighed. "And you love me, truly love me?"

Rex silenced her with a lingering kiss. Clarissa sighed, coughed up a little dirt, and rested her head on Rex's chest. "Will you love me forever, dearest?" she asked.

Rex, choked with emotion, could barely respond. "Until the cows come home, my love."

THE END

DEAD MEN
DON'T
BREATHE

BY JOE SPINDLE

CHAPTER 5

*Dead Men Don't Breathe
By Joe Spindle*

1 It still eats at me. I can deal with it a little better now, but it still eats at me. It's not like the old days when all it took was a sharp mind, quick hand and a big gun. A Joe could walk the streets and earn a decent living by being streetwise and knowing the right people. In those days when people tried to kill you, they were physical about it. They would blow up your car or try to gun you down in the street. At least you had a fighting chance. All you needed was your .45 and nerves of steel.

Now they kill you in ways you can't even see. A little at a time. At first you don't even know it's happening. Then, boom, one day you're in a cage made of wires, disks and paper trying to figure out how to turn the damn thing off. Maybe it's time I retired and moved to Florida. I hear that they don't get so upset down there if you happen to blow away someone who's mugging a little old lady.

Zelda took to the machine like a duck to water. When she's working with it, you hear music playing. Sometimes the music is so damn loud that I have to tell her to turn the radio down. I have to admit that the work she does with the machine has helped us solve many cases, but the machine and I just don't seem to get along. With Zelda there seems to be a cosmological relationship between her and the bucket of bolts. She can hook up with almost any computer in the world and it will play her tune. Sometimes she is so deep into that mechanical moocher that she doesn't even notice my coming and going at the office. I even have to get my own coffee.

Zelda put one of those damn machines into my office saying, "Hey, Joe, it's time to get with the future. You don't want to be left behind do you?" Well, maybe I do want to be left behind. There is more to life than a television that can't even play an "I Love Lucy" rerun.

I spill coffee on the keyboard. Zelda gets it fixed. I accidentally put a .45 slug through the computer TV while I was doing the 4:30 p.m. cleaning of my baby. Zelda gets it fixed. I put a cheese sandwich in the disk drive for safe keeping. Zelda gets it fixed. Zelda has trouble dealing with subtle messages.

I called Jack just to see what was up. Jack's now the Chief of Police, a big step up from the days when he was a captain in homicide. Now he gets all the dope on all of the cases.

"Chief of Police."

"You love saying that, don't you Jack?"

"What do you want, Joe? You know how busy I am."

"Yeah, right! What are you doing, reviewing the latest computer printout of police expense accounts?"

"These computers drive me crazy. They can generate more paper than a whole troop of police chiefs are able to review. I never look at the reports because no sane person would be able to understand them. I just save them until I have enough paper to recycle. You can get about $250 a ton for computer paper. It'll make a nice supplement to my retirement."

"It must feel great to be making such a significant contribution to society."

"Cut the crap, Joe! How about coming down to city hall. I'll take you to lunch. I may have something that will interest you."

"I don't know if I can make it. I have a program to debug on my computer."

"Cut the crap, Joe!"

"I'll be down in 15 minutes." I hung up the phone and hopped over the desk accidentally knocking the computer TV off the machine.

"Oops!" I muttered just as Zelda walked into the office.

"You're hopeless, Joe." Zelda scolded in her sternest voice. At least as stern as she could be considering the years we had been together and all the times we had wanted to touch each other and hadn't.

Yes, we had a special relationship. A little weird, but special. I didn't want to touch her until we had tied the knot, but every time we would set the date something would come up. Once the preacher disappeared. Once, the night before the wedding, the church burned down. Another time, Zelda was kidnapped by the mob. The last time, while Zelda stood waiting at the church, I was sitting in jail after blowing away some Commie pig. But Zelda was patient with me. We hadn't set the next date yet.

"What do mean hopeless? It wasn't my fault that Commie pig tried to blow me away. The cops were there before I knew it and I couldn't get out in time for the ceremony."

"I'm talking about the computer. You're not giving it a chance."

"Oh that. It was an accident." She used to be able to read my mind. I wondered if we were growing apart.

As I walked out the door I glanced at Zelda and her body, the body that any man would have died to touch. Come to think of it many men had died without touching it. They were always staring at her. I knew what they were thinking. I had often thought the same thing myself. All it took was my .45 to set them straight. Something told me that I'd better walk a little faster if I hoped to avoid Zelda's temptation. God, I loved that woman.

"See you later, Zelda."

"It doesn't look like you broke the monitor, thank God." Zelda yelled after me.

"Yeah, right. I'll do better next time." I muttered to myself.

When I hit the front steps, I felt the refreshing burn of the exhaust fumes of the daily traffic. There was something about the smell of the city which was comforting. Maybe it was the knowledge that if a bullet from someone's rod didn't kill me, the smog would. Anything would be better than suffocating in a pile of computer printouts. I retched slightly as I passed some garbage cans. The garbage men had been on strike for two months, which definitely contributed to the city's atmosphere.

I noticed a man pulling a dog down the sidewalk, giving an occasional tug to get the mutt away from the garbage cans. It was a cute little animal who obviously wanted to investigate everything in its path ... not unlike myself. The man kept yanking at the leash and yelling at the canine. I couldn't take it anymore.

"Dogs are people, too."

In a flash I pulled out my .45 and swung it across the side of the man's head—laying him out over a rail and down some steps. The dog just kept sniffing one of the nearby cans. Walking down the steps, I grabbed this animal-hater by the collar and pulled him to his feet while throwing him against the wall. He groaned to show that I had his attention. The pooch trotted up to me wagging its tail with curiosity and began sniffing.

"If I ever catch you treating that stupid mutt that way again, I'll blow your brains all over the wall with this .45! Remember, dogs are people, too!"

I released the degenerate's collar, letting him sink to the ground, pushed the canine off my leg, and went on my merry way. It turns my stomach to see people who think they are the only people in the world. If we let people treat animals like animals, where will it stop? Next we will be treating plants like animals, not to mention insects and amphibians.

Of course, in my heart, what was left of it, I knew that I was no better than any of them, but that was what made me so good. I was one of them and knew it. But they didn't know that I knew it. That gave me the edge. I started whistling. Then I started skipping. Then I played a quick game of hopscotch that was drawn in chalk on the sidewalk by some kids. People were staring.

I pulled out my .45 and yelled, "Whhaaat?" They went about their business.

I arrived at Jack's office 14 minutes after I had hung up the phone. I like to be punctual. Jack was kicking back, reading a newspaper with his feet propped on his desk.

"Anything good in the comics?" I jabbed.

"Joe! It's good to see you. I'm starved. Let's go get a greasy taco." Jack spit out these words as he jumped up and grabbed his coat all in one quick motion. He had always been quick. Not quick in a mental way, but in a physical way. He had played football in high school and would have been all-state if that incident with the cheerleader hadn't happened. He got kicked off the team and never said a word about it. Which was a good thing because I was the one who actually caused the problem with the cheerleader. But Jack was such a good friend he never turned me in. I owed him one.

"I'll buy, Jack," I offered. How else can you repay a guy who destroyed his boyhood dreams of going pro just so his friend could keep his name out of the school newspaper. "But only the small taco, and none of that sour cream or green stuff, either."

"That's okay, Joe. I'm buying today."

Whew! That was a close one. But now that SOB was going to hold that cheerleader thing over my head for the rest of my life. I grabbed an M&M off his desk and followed him out the door.

After we finished off a couple of greasy tacos with green stuff, Jack just sat there with a dour look on his face. I figured that it was the green stuff repeating on him. But it might be worse. There could be internal explosions going off in his abdomen like the popping of a .22 caliber peashooter. Or who knows?

"Joe, I need some help," Jack whispered as he leaned toward me.

I grabbed him quick and started to drag him toward the restroom. I didn't want to be embarrassed, even in a dive like this.

"No, no, Joe! It isn't that!"

I released my grip on his arm and said, "It would be understandable. I'm repeating a little myself." I felt sure that he was going to bring up that cheerleader thing.

As we sat down again, Jack said, "I have a problem and I think you're probably the only who can help me." He didn't say anything about the cheerleader. Maybe it would be better if I just let the issue drop.

Jack continued, "We have this sting operation going, but some things have gone wrong and I need a new face, someone who isn't connected with the police department, to do some investigating. Someone like you."

"I'm not sure that you can say I'm not connected with the police department. I did go to the Policeman's Ball one year with Zelda and, come to think of it, I went in disguise as your date one year. I even had to shave my moustache and we were voted the loveliest couple, which earned me a bouquet of roses. And what about the picnic I went to?"

"Yeah, I forgot about those, but I think you can still do this job, Joe."

"And what about the time …"

"Joe!" interrupted Jack. "Do you want the job or not?"

"Well, I don't know. How much does it pay? Will I get a opportunity to meet a gorgeous blonde who will seduce me in her apartment? Do I get to shoot anyone? Will it make me a national hero? Will I get my picture in the newspaper?"

"It doesn't pay a cent, but you may get all those other things."

"Well, okay. As long as I don't have to use a computer."

"You might have to use a computer, Joe."

"No way, Jose! I'm not touching no stinking computer!"

"We'll throw in a rich brunette who wears dresses that fit like a glove and an extra Commie pig for blowing away."

"Well . . . okay. What's the deal?"

In soft tones, Jack started to give me the background. I listened intently, while trying to control the rumbling in my stomach from the two greasy tacos with green stuff. "About two years ago, the department, under my guidance, set up a dummy organization to infiltrate other criminal organizations. It was designed to be a massive sting bringing down all of the bigwigs in organized crime. The idea was to pretend to commit crimes that would give other crime organizations confidence in us. Then we would join forces with real organized crime families, eventually infiltrating our way to the top. Once at the top, we would pull off the sting, arresting all the national crime bosses. Pretty clever, huh?"

I grunted as I built a little pile of green stuff on the side of my plate.

Jack continued, "Everything was progressing beautifully. When the real crime bosses first put out a contract to hit someone, we rented an old hotel with a swimming pool in the country and disappeared the target to the hotel. The family bosses thought the target was dead, while the victim lived in comfort at the hotel. To date, we have about 75 victims holed up and living in style. Our credibility is high with the families. They've awarded us with a Triple-A rating for murder. We take pride in our professionalism and that award.

"When we participated in a drug deal we would buy all of the drugs ourselves. When we robbed a bank we would fund that with government money. In prostitution, we provided both the hookers and the johns. They would just play pinochle all night long. Our operation has grown so much that it employs about 20,000 people throughout the country. We are one of the biggest, if not *the* biggest crime organizations in the country. It's been tremendously expensive and, now, the big boys are expecting some results.

"We're almost ready to deliver those results. The plan has worked so well that we have our top man actually sitting on the Secret Family Crime Bosses Council. The Crime Bosses Council members are the most notorious crime bosses in the country. Our man on the inside has been able to collect extensive information.

"Here's the problem, Joe. About two months ago, we were ready to bring down the sting. Our top guy, being a member of the secret council, was in the process of getting the final pieces of information before launching the sting, when, as of two weeks ago, he dropped out of sight. You can guess what's happened to him."

I realized it could only mean one thing, "He's dead, 6-feet under, gone West, buried, never to return or be heard from again, deceased, perished, defunct, lifeless, inanimate, obsolete, extinct, obliterated, annihilated, destroyed, extinguished, removed, departed, passed away, gave up the ghost, walked the plank, bit the dust, checked out, croaked, popped off, took a ride, signed off, cashed in his chips." I slid the pile of green stuff to the other side of my plate.

"Yeah, that's our guess too," continued Jack. "Anyway, we have to get someone back on the inside. It's all set up for someone the crime bosses have never met to take his place on the council, but it will be extremely dangerous for this person."

"Who's this person?" I asked.

"You, Joe." My hand twitched, causing my fork to knock the little pile of green stuff off my plate into my lap.

I smiled. Back in action, at the heart of the problem, the focal point, reaching the marrow, interjacent, in the thick of it. Yes, smack dab in the middle of it all. That's where I belonged. I could get all the names Jack needed to bring the whole thing down. And so what if I didn't; I'd just blow them all away. I could feel my .45 glowing, warming my arm. We were communicating. We knew each other and believed in each other. The heat was so strong that my deodorant started to break down.

"You can depend on me, Jack."

"Great, Joe! It's just that there isn't anyone else I can afford to lose. Er . . . I mean at this moment. What with the annual budget review and all my good people on computers day and night."

"Poor slobs!" I thought to myself. I would take the heat any day to avoid the agony of battling one of those mindless machines. They weren't worth a bullet from a cheap Saturday Night Special.

Well, at least Jack didn't bring up the thing about the cheerleader. Of course, I could feel the green stuff from the greasy taco about to come up, so I quickly made my exit to the restroom.

When I returned, Jack gave me an invitation to the next meeting of the Secret Family Crime Boss Council. "Show this at the door and it will identify you as the new man for our organization."

"Do I need any phony IDs or a password?" I inquired.

"No."

"Are there any special signs that I should know?"

"No."

"Will I need money for lunch?"

"No, that's all taken care of. Just show up and they'll know who you are."

"Jack, this seems a little bit too easy. Will they frisk me at the door."

"No. Everyone wears a gun there, so they will expect you to wear one too. It's considered part of meeting attire."

"That's convenient."

"Don't worry, Joe. The bond between these ruthless crime families is so tight you'll be able to move freely. They operate on trust within their own organizations. It's amazing, but they actually seem quite ethical. If they weren't such filthy slime, they would actually be quite nice people to work with."

They didn't seem like my kind of people. Were we getting a better quality criminal these days? Did they drink tea and eat crumpets? Did they hold polite conversation with their victims before they blew them away? It turned my stomach. I longed for the good old days when you could tell slime by their smell. I was going to take a particular pleasure in unloading a few clips of .45 bullets into this crowd.

"Thanks, Jack. I'll give you a call as soon I can."

"You better, Joe! I don't want you leaving me hanging like you did with the cheerleader in high school!"

I knew he couldn't leave that cheerleader thing alone. I felt my stomach tie into a knot. I made a dash for the restroom. It was the green stuff again. When I returned Jack, was gone.

2 I caught a cab up to the *Daily Herald Tribune Examiner Post* building to talk to my crime reporter buddy Joe Whiplash. We had always maintained what you would call a mutually beneficial relationship. I would give him hot stories and he would give me background for my investigations. I knew that anything that could be known about this Evil Secret Family Crime Bosses Council would be known by Joe.

At the reception desk sat a big, beautiful, buxom blonde with a mohair sweater so tight it made her eyes bulge. I've always had a thing for bulging eyes. She was sitting behind a computer squinting at the TV tube while mumbling to herself. The mohair on her sweater was standing on end and pointing in the direction of the computer TV. I could see that there was something electrical here. She finally looked up, almost knocking me out with her toothy smile. I picked myself up off the floor and asked where I could find Joe.

"Who should I say is calling?" she asked in a soft, seductive tone that showed she could control any situation.

"Just tell Joe it's Joe, Baby."

She picked up the phone and dialed a short number. "Joe? Joe Baby is here to see you."

"No, the name is Joe Screwdriver, Baby," I interjected.

"His name is Joe Screwdriver Baby. Should I send him up?" After a few moments of conversation the blonde turned to me and said that Joe would be right down. I could tell that she wanted me. But I was on a case. There was no time to fool around. At least, not in this chapter.

"Maybe next time I'll show you a good time," I offered as I was waiting for Joe.

"What?" she asked as she looked up for the computer. "Did you say something?"

At that moment, out of the corner of my eye, I saw the end of a rifle sticking out of the stairwell. My reflexes were instantaneous. I had my .45 in hand and squeezed off two rounds into the stairwell. One hit the barrel of the rifle and the other slapped into the wall. The rifle went tumbling to the ground and everyone in the lobby, except me, hit the deck. From around the corner I heard, "Joe? Is that you, Joe?"

It was Joe. He had picked up a toy rifle for his kid and was bringing it down to show me how realistic it looked.

"You could have fooled me. In fact you did fool me. Sorry about that, but you know how I get when I'm on a case."

"Will this case mean a story for me, Joe?" asked Joe.

"It could. What can you tell me about it?"

"You have to tell me something first before I can give you anything," demanded Joe.

"I went first last time. It always seems like I have to go first. It's your turn this time," I demanded.

"Okay, okay! How about this? Two weeks ago they pulled Joe Franco's body out of the river. They took him down to the city morgue and did an autopsy. It was unbelievable. The autopsy showed that Joe wasn't dead at all. He was only holding his breath."

"Joe, wasn't Joe a runner for one of the organizations?" I asked.

"Yes, Joe, I think it was the YMCA," Joe filled in.

"How is he tied into the Slimy Secret Family Bosses Crime Council?" I asked.

"Joe, you have a story on the Stinky Secret Family Crime Bosses Council? You have to give it to me. You just have to. I haven't had a good story in such a long time that I could just spit."

I jumped out of the way just in case. "First you tell me how Joe Franco ties in."

Joe continued, "I don't know that he does. I just gave you that story to get you talking and to hold up my end of the conversation."

A feeling rose in the pit of my stomach. I knew in my gut that Joe Franco was somehow tied into this case. But how? The pieces just didn't add up. The numbers didn't fit. How could someone hold their breath that long? Even more important: Why? The queasiness in my tummy was growing. I knew I was on to something. Of course, it could have been the two tacos with green stuff that I had for lunch. "Tell me what you know about the Secret Crime council, Joe," I demanded.

"There's not much to tell. Everything seems to be shrouded in mystery. There are a few mumblings here and there, but nothing you could hang your hat on. I've thrown out feelers, but they all seem to come back blank. Every time I try to check things out I run into a brick wall. Nobody's talking. It's either because they're scared or they don't know anything. When I go to the well on this subject the well is dry, bone dry. If information were the hair on my head, I would be bald."

"You are bald, Joe," I noted.

"That explains it, Joe. Will you give me the story before it breaks?"

"Does a bear eat pasta?" I mumbled as I walked out the door. As usual I had wasted my time by talking to a reporter. They were all the same. They never knew anything worth knowing. Social parasites! Social parasites of the worst kind! Well, not the worst kind. Bankers were worse. They wouldn't even give a business man a little loan for a new .45. Of course, bankers aren't as bad as stockbrokers. Stockbrokers should go out and get real jobs, so they can hold their heads high in public. Now, stockbrokers aren't as bad as lawyers. They should all be shot, and I'm just the man to do it.

It made me thankful that I only dealt with honest criminals, crooks who openly robbed or murdered people. None of those social parasites who, like leeches, sucked you dry while smiling and holding your hand. It turned my stomach.

As I was walking down the street, I noticed a stunningly beautiful woman in a fur coat on the other side of the street. Suddenly it clicked and I had to get over to her as quick as possible. Running across the street, I dodged a couple of cars that blasted their horns, but I didn't have time to stop and teach them manners. I had to reach her before it was too late. She was about to turn the corner when I caught her from behind.

I ripped off her coat and threw it to the ground. She stumbled and fell to the sidewalk. As she stared up at me, I could see the fear in her eyes as they darted in bewilderment. Her hands trembled, opening her purse and reaching inside. I kicked the purse away. "Don't you know that it's cruel to make coats out of poor defenseless bunny rabbits?" I snarled through my clenched teeth. I could see a change in her expression. I knew that my message was getting across. "Bunny rabbits are people, too."

This beautiful babe slowly raised herself off the ground, gritted her teeth and said, "This is a fake fur coat made from petroleum by-products."

I looked at her. I looked at the coat. I looked at her again and then again the coat. I seemed to be in a pretty sticky situation. I could feel the tacos again. As I picked up the coat, I commented, "It sure looks real."

I dusted off the coat and handed it to the woman who was now steaming, all fear gone. The radiating heat told me she didn't need the coat for warmth at this moment. I reached for the purse, which she accepted with a yank, quickly opening it, taking out her compact and a bottle of mace. Before I knew what was happening it was mace in my face and a knee in my... ugh... well, you know. I quickly relinquished my upright stance for a fetal position on the sidewalk where I could better protect myself while recovering from the shock and the pain. Through the mace haze I could see her freshening up with her compact while occasionally glancing down at me with a smug smile. I could tell she liked me. She turned on her heel and left me there to die. I crawled to a pay phone and dialed the office.

"Hello, Screwdriver Investigations," answered Zelda.

"Zelda, this is Joe," I rasped out.

"Joe! What's the matter? You sound like you were just kicked in the ... ugh ... well, you know."

"I know that all too well, Baby." I was beginning to recover. "I want you to get on your computer and check something out for me."

"Anything for you, Joe. You know how I miss you. When are you coming back to the office? I have so much to tell you. Do you remember Cindy Lukas? The one who works down the hall? Well, she was telling me that a friend of hers had met this really good-looking guy. She says that he sort of looks like a cross between Robert Redford, Paul Newman and PeeWee Herman. He's absolutely gorgeous. Anyway, they were planning on going out to dinner at Mr. Alfonso's Italian Food when ..."

Now, I remembered why Zelda and I hadn't gotten married yet. I slowly eased myself off the floor of the telephone booth while listening to all the details of the romance of the friend of Cindy

Lukas who works down the hall. Cindy, not the friend. I occasionally threw in an "Uh-huh" or a "Yeah" while looking for an opening to end it all. Sometimes a guy just has to be tough and I was toughing this one out.

I watched the people walk by, earnest in their personal destinations. I scanned the traffic as it stopped at a nearby traffic light. I carefully counted all the red cars. The sun was slowly creeping behind the buildings. I could never go out of town to work. I wouldn't be able to afford the telephone bills. Then, I heard my opening.

"… and it turned out she was pregnant. What do you think about that?"

"Zelda, I want you find out everything you can on a guy named Joe Franco. They pulled him out of the river a couple of weeks ago and it turned out he was alive, just holding his breath."

"Of course, Joe. Right away. You know that I would do anything for you. I'm more dedicated to you then Cindy's girlfriend is to her handsome boyfriend. Even though she is pregnant, she has an eye for this other guy who lives one floor up from her …"

I handed the telephone receiver to a derelict walking by and went on my way. I had a Rotten Secret Family Crime Bosses Council meeting to go to and didn't want to be the last one there. I knew Zelda would be well taken care of. That woman was my whole life and I wanted her to be happy. I figured the derelict would give her some stimulating conversation. All he had to do was listen.

When, I reached the location of the Loathsome Secret Family Crime Council meeting, the sun was just setting behind a sleazy old bar across the street that used to be a hangout for investment bankers and other low-lifes. In the old days, Zelda would go there and pick up junk bonds for her mother. I stood there and mulled over in my head the kind of sludge who would sell junk bonds to unsuspecting junk-bond junkies. They should all be forced to watch golf on television for one solid week.

I turned to enter the broken down tenement where my meeting was to be held. Two apes stood by the door in trench coats. The lumps under their arms were the size of bowling balls, indicating that they were either packing an arsenal or a malignant growth.

As I tried to pass, one of the trench coats grabbed my arm. I swung my elbow straight up under his chin, knocking his head back with a jerk. His head fell off and rolled down the street. Then a little voice from inside the trench coat asked, "Do you have an invitation?" as a gun emerged from between the buttons and jammed into my side. This was weird. Clever, but weird.

I, carefully, pulled the invitation out of my pocket and handed it to the other trenchcoat. "He looks okay to me," he responded after scrutinizing the invite. "Go on in," he motioned while returning the invitation. The other trenchcoat put away his gun and hobbled down the street after his head. Weird.

Inside there was a big, beautiful, buxom blonde sitting behind a reception desk with glasses on so tight it made her sweater bulge. I always liked blondes with glasses. She studied my invitation, then directed me up a set of stairs to a dark, little smoke-filled room.

There was something odd about the room. It seemed normal enough, especially for a meeting like this, but it just didn't feel right. The family crime bosses were there: four people, two men and two women, dressed in business suits. So these were the scumbag crime bosses who planned and organized the evil in this country and, probably, the world. It all seemed too simple. Was it really that easy to get into the sewer rat's inner circle or was this just a first hurdle?

The man closest to me walked up with his hand outstretched to introduce himself. "I'm Charlie Davis. You must be the new guy on the secret council." This was too easy. The guy was ugly, but too friendly.

"Yeah, I'm Joe Screwdriver. How are you doing?" I smiled. It was the smile I give just before blowing off some punk's head. Charlie smiled back as if he hadn't noticed my devastating smile. He then proceeded to introduce the other crime bosses.

There was Susan Smith. She was a brunette about five-foot-six with a tiny mole on her right cheek. She moved with the self-confidence that you would expect from a madame in a brothel. I wondered which family she ran and what kind of crime they were into. Maybe her name wasn't really Smith. Could she be the notorious Susarullio Gambabinorino? She eyed me with that stare that makes you wonder if there's a piece of spinach stuck between your teeth.

Jim Phillips was the other male family boss. His sinewy muscles clung to his clothes in the way that drives women crazy. His wavy brown hair and deep blue eyes would have made him any woman's dream date. He was just macho enough, yet not too mucho macho. He moved like a cat and exuded an air of superiority over other men, while demanding submission and devotion from women. I was going to take great pleasure in blowing this male bimbo's head off. I wondered if he might be Mick Paddy O'Neil, the crime boss famous for running the Boston Marathon backwards.

Cathy Carmichal was the other female, if you can use that word. She was short and fat and had pimples. My guess was that she ate pizza every night. I could smell the garlic from across the room. I wondered how she got into this story. I wasn't used to working with broads who weren't good-lookers. This one was definitely made to be behind a computer. Who else would have her? I shook her hand, then wiped it on my coat. This could ruin my reputation.

Charlie had finished the intros. He wasn't such a sharp dresser. I think he and Cathy must have bought their clothes at the same store ... off the same rack. His glasses were partially fogged from the smoke in the room. His deodorant had given out years ago. He had sopping pits that went from his wrists to his waist. I could see

Jim and Susan on an important and very evil council like this, but Charlie and Cathy just didn't fit the image and I didn't feel comfortable about having them in my story. I would have to replace them. But how?

We all sat down at the table to begin the meeting. I pulled out a pack of smokes and was about to light up when I noticed that there were no ashtrays on the table. Hesitating, I asked, "Mind if I smoke?"

"Actually, we do," responded Cathy. "It's filthy habit and we wish that you would quit."

Bitch. I was going to have to get her out of this story.

Suddenly, I knew what was wrong with the room. It was smoke filled, yet no one smoked. "Where did all this smoke come from?"

"What smoke?" asked Charlie.

Then I realized that it was the lingering effects of the mace. This wasn't my day. And now I couldn't even have a smoke. I heard the green stuff from the greasy taco rumble in my stomach.

The conversation was dull and fatuous. Now I knew what had happened to my predecessor. The crime bosses had bored him to death. My mind wandered while they droned on. How did Joe Franco tie in? How could anyone hold their breath that long? Where was Jimmy Hoffa? Why did Socrates take the poison? Was Plato really gay? Did Shakespeare actually write all of those plays? Is charbroiled better than fried? What kind of pansy would drink non-alcoholic beer?

Eventually, all the bosses stood and approached a door in the back of the room. As Charlie opened the door I could see some flashes of light breaking through the opening. My instincts took over and I was pure animal reaction. As I dove through the door, I simultaneously reached for my .45, pulling it to full extension, cocked. Before I hit the floor boards in a prone position, I had squeezed off two rounds, each impacting their separate target with deadly accuracy. I rattled off three more shots at the remaining targets, each exploding upon impact. With the exception of a few sparks and crackles the room had gone quiet. The collision with

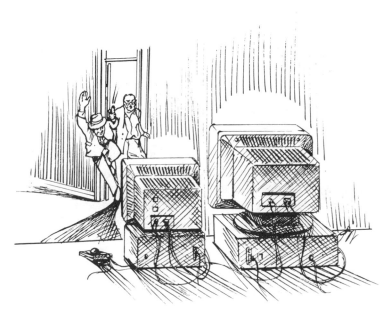

"As Charlie opened the door I could see some flashes of light through the opening."

the floor had knocked the wind out of me and only my gasping could be heard over the electrical hisses.

I slowly rolled over to see the four bosses staring with bug eyes, mouths hanging open. Cathy Carmichal had a bit of drool at the corner of her mouth. "You destroyed our computers," Cathy spit. "These are the terminals we use to control the families." All four continued to gawk in disbelief. Five computer TVs were destroyed, each with a bullet precisely centered from the barrel of my baby.

As I regained my wind, I slowly leveled and raised myself while holstering my .45. "Sorry about that, I thought it was a trap." I wasn't a damn bit sorry. Anything that put a kink in their business was okay by me. They were shocked and angry.

I wiped Cathy's spit off my clothes and quickly gathered up the keyboards, saying, "I'll have these things checked out and get them back tomorrow." They were buying my story. They didn't suspect me at all. They bought the cover. They just put all my actions down to stupidity.

I took off with the keyboards. When I hit the front steps the trench coats were gone.

3 I dropped the keyboards off with Jack so he could have them checked for fingerprints. With the names of the Odious Secret Family Bosses Crime Council members and fingerprints he would be able to check out these jokers. I also asked Jack to get the lowdown on Joe Franco. I just couldn't see where Joe Franco fit in. While I was at it, I asked Jack to have Cathy Carmichal removed from this story. She was just too ugly for me—maybe one of his hits or something.

I caught a cab to the office. Zelda was waiting at her computer.

"I have some info on Joe Franco, Joe."

"Okay, yeah, let's hear it."

"It seems that he has a long record of trouble with the police. Mostly for holding his breath in public. He's been arrested a number of times for causing public disturbances: fake drownings, conspicuous redface, budging veins, that sort of thing. He's a real crusader. He feels that it is everyone's inalienable right to hold their breath anywhere they want, whenever they want."

"Zelda, I'm as open-minded as the next Joe, but some things just go too far. I don't mind if people hold their breath in the privacy of their own home—for as long as they want. But when they start imposing their belief system on everyone else by doing it in public, well, that's too much. We're not Commies here.

"What if everyone started holding their breath? Who would make the carbon dioxide for the trees to survive? If the trees died, who would make oxygen for people to survive? These crazies just don't think of the long-range implications of their actions. Don't people know that trees are people too?"

As I looked around I noticed that Zelda had left the room. God, how I loved that woman. Just as I was about to think some long, rambling, inane thoughts about Zelda, the phone rang.

"Joe speaking," I stated as I slammed the receiver against my ear, almost rupturing my eardrum.

"This is Jack."

"No, this is Joe. Jack is the Chief of Police, and a damned fine one if I do say so myself."

"No Joe! This *is* Jack speaking, the Chief of Police!"

I got the message. "You sure do like to brag, don't you, Jack?"

"Shut up and listen, Joe! We sent the prints in for ID and they came up blank."

"You mean there were no prints on the keyboards?"

"No, there were plenty of prints. They just weren't on file anywhere. The Feds have nothing. The state has nothing. It's just one big blank. The members of the secret council are well covered. There's more. When I sent their names in a lot of people started getting very interested. I've got Feds snooping around here asking questions, but not giving any answers of their own. The state police are doing the same thing only they don't trust the Feds either. I think that we may be onto something that's being covered up by the upper echelons. I'm worried that our entire governmental structure may be infiltrated by the secret council. There is even a guy from the phone company wandering around asking questions about Joe Franco."

"My God, don't tell me that Ma Bell is involved in this thing."

"I don't have any evidence, but it sure smells bad."

"Try opening the window, Jack. That usually helps. Do you have anything on Joe Franco?"

"That's strange too, Joe. Other than the things Zelda told you at the beginning of this chapter, this isn't much else to say."

"Well, that will save some time—and some redundant writing."

"But when I mentioned Joe Franco to the Feds and state police, they got very interested. They were very hush hush on all the other names, but wouldn't stop asking questions about Joe Franco. They wanted to know everything we knew about him. They got me so hyped up that I decide to have Joe picked up, Joe."

"That sounds like a good idea ..." As I was about to ask another question, the phone slipped out of my hand and crashed to the floor. The line had disconnected. After I returned the receiver to the phone, and before I could lift it again to order pizza, the phone rang.

When I lifted the phone and began an apology to Jack for dropping it, "You must be confused. This is Susan Smith from the secret council," came singing across the line instead.

I dropped to my knees, muffling the receiver against my chest, saying, "Thank God, it's not the ugly one!" Rising to my feet I whispered into the phone, "Excuse me; I thought you were someone else."

"Joe, I have to see you right away. Why are you whispering?"

"Sure, how about in 15 minutes down at the Blue Boy Urchin? And I wasn't whispering."

"See you then, Joe. You were, too."

"Was not." Damn! She had already hung up the phone.

About this time I was beginning to wonder if this were really a computer-related story. After all, anyone reading this book would expect it to relate to computers. But then, at this point, anyone who was still reading this story probably wouldn't care if it was computer related or not. I certainly didn't care because after all I didn't like computers anyway. Computers were Zelda's thing and, God, how I loved that woman.

It took me 45 minutes to get to the Blue Boy Urchin. My roller skates kept popping off my shoes and I had to stop to adjust them five times. Zelda kept telling me to get shoe skates, but I felt that they would ruin the shine on my wingtips.

When I walked in, Susan was sitting in a corner booth with two drinks in front of her. One was empty. As I looked around the place I noticed a number of men looking our way. This was no surprise since Susan was such a good looker. At least these goons hadn't bothered her. Something told me that she could take care of herself. As I sat down across the table from Susan, these jokers just kept staring at her. I wondered if they were going to try something.

"Joe, I know you're a private cop."

"How did you find that out? Look in the Yellow Pages?" I retorted to show my lack of concern and macho demeanor.

"Yes, as a matter of fact. Joe, I want to hire you."

"To do what? You have an entire family of low-lifes working for you, Susan. You don't need me"

"I don't want the Family to know about this one. I need to find Joe Franco and here's $5,000 for you to do it."

Five Gs. That's how I always make my money. Someone comes along and gives me money for doing something I was doing anyway. Sometimes two people offer me money, but I can't take it from both. My ethics wouldn't permit it. Ethics are very important to the professional. For example, I would never blow the face off a pretty woman. That wouldn't be ethical. An ugly one, sure, but not a pretty one.

I knew that Jack was already on his way to pick up Joe Franco, so I pocketed the cash.

We were about to leave when one of the biggest goons in the place approached our table. I reached into my coat and rested my palm on the butt of my .45, a precaution against trouble. The goon—unshaven, with a protruding beer belly and pants that hung so low his cheeks showed—turned to me and said, "Hey, buddy, you wanna dance?"

The steam hissed from under my collar. I could feel the anger building inside me. It was all so clear now. They weren't looking at Susan at all. *They were looking at me!* As flattered as I was, I felt stupid for coming here in the first place. How did I get into this position? A big, fat, smelly goon was hanging over me and I had to decide whether to blow him away, pistol whip him, take him apart with my fists, or ….

I turned to him with my face set and said, "Sure, but just one dance. I have to get someplace." I couldn't bear to hurt his feelings. After all, he didn't know I was straight.

For his size, he was pretty light on his feet and not a half-bad dancer. When the dance was over, Susan was gone.

4 Next morning, I returned to the location of the Secret Crime council meetings for our next scheduled encounter. The appointed hour had been posted at the YMCA for those who had trouble remembering when the next meeting would be. I had picked up the keyboards from Jack and carried them under my arm.

Jack was pretty worried about the whole situation and cautioned me to be careful. He felt that all hell was about to break loose and he was ready to set the whole sting operation in motion. If Jack didn't hear from me by 1:33 in the morning, he'd call in the troops. I mentioned that 1:33 in the morning was a pretty odd time and he responded, "That's the beauty of it. We will have surprise on our side. If we did it at midnight, one o'clock, one-thirty, or even on the quarter hour, they would be expecting us. But no one would expect us at 1:33 a.m."

It's hard to argue with logic like that. "Besides, Venus moves into the same house as Jupiter at that time," Jack added. I just assumed that those were code names for a couple of the undercover agents.

When I arrived at the Secret Crime Council meeting place, it was abandoned. It looked like there had been a scuffle. Everyone was gone. I cautiously removed my .45 from its holster and edged up the side of the stairs, holding the gun against the wall in front of me. As I moved into the meeting room, I dropped the keyboards onto the table. There was light coming from the door in the back of the room. Had they replaced those computers so quickly?

As I edged into the back room, I was amazed to see that all five computers were up and running. They even had keyboards. I wished that someone had told me. It would have saved me a stop at the police station. The computers were flashing numbers and symbols on their screens. I wished that Zelda were with me. She would have known what it all meant.

For that matter, where the hell was Zelda? I hadn't seen her since she had left the office earlier that day. If this were the usual case, I would later find her tied-up naked somewhere. It was the only time I ever got to see her naked. She never seemed to be around when I needed her. Oh, well, I would just have to figure these computers out myself.

I sat down behind one of the displays and started reading the symbols and numbers which were zooming by. "IBM ... FBI ... CBS ... ATT ... UPS ... CIA ... CHP ..." It was all gibberish, yet in the back of my mind it seemed to make sense. Had the government been infiltrated by the Families? Was I already too late to win this war? Had it all gone too far to stop? Not yet. Not as long as I was still alive. I knew how they thought and I could take them all apart—one at a time or all together. Well, maybe not all together, but a bunch of them at once ... as long as there weren't more than ten or 15 of them. I knew them because I was one of them.

I sat in front of another computer and studied the images. This one had a little symbol that was being chased by little goolie monsters. There were little planes sitting off to the side and a joystick sitting on the table next to the computer. I grabbed the joystick and one of the planes took off. I pushed the button and the plane blasted one of the goolies. I realized that if I could save the little symbol from the goolies, then I could save America from this terrible, seemingly inevitable disaster.

Leaning on the joystick, I veered the plane to the left and blasted another goolie. It was all coming clear. This computer was the key to the whole problem. As I destroyed another goolie, I knew that I had the case solved. I was going to save America.

The goon turned to me and asked, "Hey, buddy, you wanna dance?"

Then everything went black. Was I being swallowed by a goolie? There was shaking and rattling. It was cold and I was bouncing. It was black and my head ached. Where the hell was Zelda? Then it slowly started to clear. I was on a death ride. I reached for my .45, but found my arms bound behind my back. My left arm was underneath my body and numb from lack of circulation. As I laid there I realized that my holster was flat from the weight of my body. It was empty. They had my gun. This was so depressing.

I was in the trunk of a car speeding down some back road: destination death. I would be dumped out in the woods and have the back of my head blown off. Or would they shoot me in the heart? Maybe they would bury me alive. They could always strangle me with the rope which was pressing against my face. I'd often heard of people being beaten to death with a tire iron, similar to the one which went with the car jack which was digging into my side.

Of course, you don't have to worry about me being killed, because if I were killed, I wouldn't be able to tell you this story right now. Just so you don't get too worried, I didn't actually get killed, I just thought I was going to be killed. Now, Zelda could be killed because she's not telling the story. Or, for that matter, Jack, Susan Smith, Jim Phillips and, hopefully, Cathy Carmichal could already be dead. You see, they are all eligible for death. That's what makes it exciting for me, too. I wondered if Joe Franco were dead.

Shortly thereafter, I passed out again. This time, I thought I had died.

* * * * * * * * * * * *

When I awoke I was in a clean, bright hotel room. A bowl of fruit was next to the bed, and a chocolate on the nightstand. If this were death, I had gone to heaven.

I eased myself out of bed and stumbled to the window. Out the window, there were men and women in swimsuits lounging around an enormous pool. The women were beautiful and wearing skimpy bikinis. I had truly gone to heaven. Then I noticed that they were playing cards.

In a flood everything fell into place. They were playing pinochle. This was part of Jack's operation and they had picked up the wrong person: me. This was one of the hotels where the hookers and johns were brought to play pinochle. People who disappeared under their contracts were here. As long as I were here, I was out of action: a nobody. I had to get out.

I left the room and headed straight for the pool. Several people asked me if I would like to play pinochle. I politely declined. I strolled pass the pool and entered the woods. I picked up speed as I started running toward freedom. About 50 yards into the woods, I tripped and went flying through the air. I was momentarily stunned. I looked back and then I saw it.

At first I couldn't make it out, but as my eyes focused I saw that I had tripped over a body. It was the body of a young woman … naked. My heart raced and the pounding in my head obliterated all other sound. I could only see her back, but she was bound and gagged. I was frozen in fear that it was Zelda. Or was it Susan? I moved tentatively toward the corpse. I slowly reached for the cold shoulder and rolled the limp torso in my direction. My God! It was Zelda!

Emotion overwhelmed me. I crumpled to the ground, broken. All the years I had wasted. Why hadn't I married her? Why hadn't we moved to Florida to raise oranges? Why did it have to end this way? Where was I going to find another secretary like her? Who would make the coffee in the morning? Who would work without ever being paid?

"Gotcha!"

I looked up and there was Zelda standing there in all her naked glory laughing at me. "You fall for that one every time, Joe."

"Guess I'm just a sensitive type of guy," I sneered.

"We can't get out of here. There are hundreds of guards around the perimeter of this place." Zelda pulled her clothes and pinochle cards out of a nearby bush and put them on—the clothes, not the cards. "You should have seen the look on your face."

"Bitch," I muttered under my breath.

Zelda and I returned to the hotel. I tried to explain my situation to everyone who worked at the hotel, but they didn't care. They worked for the government and had turned into the typical bureaucrats. They showed up every day, did what they thought was their job and listened to nobody.

After a couple of months, I didn't even care. After all, I was becoming a pretty good pinochle player. The meals were decent, the beds were comfortable and we never had to rise above our present level of mediocrity. I think that I would still be there today watching "Gilligan Island" reruns if it hadn't finally fallen apart.

A career counselor came to the hotel one day and told us that we would have to be retrained to enter society. Now I definitely thought that this was part of a Commie plot. Maybe the Commies had taken over the entire country, sent every all-American to one of these hotels, and planned to brainwash us one at a time. I sure wasn't anxious to leave the hotel, especially for a brainwash. A little rinse might be okay, but not a full-cycle wash.

As it turned out, I was shipped off to a school to learn computer programming. Talk about torture. It was the worse kind of punishment. I had died and gone to hell. Then one day, who do I run into but Jack—my old buddy who had gotten me into this in the first place.

"Hey, Joe, what's going on?" Jack called to me.

"What are you doing here, Jack? A little late to spring me, isn't it?" I responded cynically.

"I'm studying computer programming, the same as you. It's really a hell of a deal."

"You've got to be kidding. The Commies are controlling everything now."

"No, Joe, you've got it all wrong. Didn't you ever get the full story on what went down?"

"All I know, Jack, is that I was hijacked to one of your hotels and you left me there to rot."

"That wasn't one of my hotels."

"What? What do mean, 'not one of your hotels'?" I was stunned.

"No, you were in one of the FBI's hotels. They were also running a sting and we didn't even know it. It was almost exactly like the one I was running. Isn't that hilarious?"

"The humor escapes me, Jack."

"Wait, it gets better. The state police also had a sting operation going in the same manner, as well as two other government agencies and one private outfit which was funded by the government. In all they figure that 1.5 million people participated in the sting operations over a period of ten years."

"With that kind of manpower, they must have really put a dent in the old crime situation."

"That's the funniest part." Jack was getting a little hysterical. "We only stung other government agencies, not the crime families at all. Every single person who was captured was acting undercover for the government somewhere. It was all for nothing."

"How did Joe Franco fit in?"

"He brought the whole thing down."

"Singled-handedly?"

"No, he didn't actually do anything. When you dropped his name with me and I started checking him out along with the names of the other members of the supposedly Notorious Secret Crime council, who, as it happens, were all undercover agents, all the government agencies started looking for Joe Franco. The newspapers got a hold of it, thinking that the government was trying to restrict Joe's right to hold his breath. Worried that the press might be getting too close to their sting operation, the FBI put their sting into action. Once one sting was set off the rest went like dominos. Everyone was scared. By the time everything settled down, agents were making simultaneous arrests of each other. The state police were rounding up FBI agents, while we were hauling in state police. It was one hell of a mess." Jack was getting nervous and excited.

"Are you okay, Jack? You're getting a little crazy."

"How would you be if you had just wasted the last ten years of your life?"

"So what's all this programming school and retraining about? Why don't they just let everyone go home?"

"Are you kidding? We can't just lay off 1.5 million government employees. That would cause a major economic depression. Their only skill is playing pinochle and the professional pinochle tour can only absorb just so many. We have to retrain these people for commercial jobs."

"Well, why retrain me? I can go back to my profession. I was doing just fine, thank you very much."

"Sorry, Joe. It turns out that most of those people you've been tracking and blowing away were government employees. Now that the stings are over there isn't much demand for your type of work."

"The papers are going to have a field day on this one."

"No, I don't think so. The stings have turned in a cover-up. Almost everyone who is anyone was involved at some level. If word ever got out it would be chaos."

"What's to stop me from telling?"

"You don't have to be stopped. Who would believe you?"

I had watched a lot of television in my day, but this was one I hadn't seen before. Trapped between the government and greasy tacos, I knew that there was little I could do. It looked like it was going to be tough for a Joe to make a living as a private cop. Zelda was getting all As in her programming class and I was barely getting C-minuses. It was never going to be the same again.

It turned my stomach.

CHAPTER 6

Fifty Things to Do While Your Spouse Is Computing

Let's face it, you have to entertain yourself somehow while your spouse is computing. But what do you do?

Not to worry. After interviewing 3,468 computer widow and widowers, we have compiled the following list of the 50 most popular things to do. Most of these things you can do by yourself, but you must use your own best judgement. We accept no liability for the outcome of any of these ideas, if you actually do them.

Advice is cheap. It's following advice that tends to be expensive.

1. Learn a foreign language like Swahili or Serbo-Croatian. The world is getting smaller.

2. Look up your high school sweetheart and guess how much weight he or she has gained since high school. Aren't you glad you broke up?

3. Change the oil in your car; drain the oil in spouse's car.

4. Organize your class reunion and go alone. Tell everyone you're divorced so they don't feel sorry for you.

5. Shampoo the carpets, except around where the computer is. Run all the floppy disks through the dishwasher. (Warning: If you do this, first go to court to get a restraining order.)

6. Re-seed the lawn. Re-seed the lawn. Re-seed the lawn.

7. Rewrite "War and Peace," correcting all the factual errors made by Tolstoy.

8. Read the classics, all of them. Do this one and you can forget the rest.

9. Start doing crossword puzzles.

10. Start a 976 telephone service. It's a good way to make new friends and earn extra income.

11. Learn Chinese cooking. Teach the Chinese American cooking.

11. Strip the wax off the kitchen floor.

12. Buy a computer for your best friend's spouse so you and your best friend can go out and party together.

13. Hold a funeral for your spouse—complete with coffin and candles. Tell your spouse you're just practicing.

14. Rent out the extra space in your spouse's head to bring in extra income.

15. Go back to school in preparation for starting a new life. This time a real life—with real people in it.

16. Buy a bigger television and put it in the same room with the computer.

17. Go bowling, drink beer and burp a lot.

18. Start watching football. Memorize the players and coaches, learning all their stats. Complain about the play-by-play people every time your spouse starts talking about computers.

19. Hide all the Doritos and pretend you know nothing about it.

20. Learn more about computers than your spouse knows, then embarrass him/her in front of other nerds.

21. Trick your spouse into coming to bed by leaving a trail of Doritos from the computer to the bedroom.

22. Buy a computer that's better than your spouse's, but don't let your spouse touch it. Don't let anyone touch it, not even you.

23. Learn computer words and throw them into the conversation at every opportunity. This is similar to name dropping, but provokes much greater respect among nerds.

24. Act more interested in the computer than in your spouse. This will cause great confusion and certainly bring about a rage of uncontrolled jealousy. You won't know whether your spouse is jealous of you or the computer, though.

25. Go to computer user-group meetings, but don't invite your spouse.

26. Learn how to take computers apart, and do it daily.

27. Go to the movies on Monday, Wednesday and Friday nights. Rent videos on Tuesday, Thursday and Sunday nights. Party Saturday nights.

28. Arrange a party for 100 people on the night that your spouse has a major computer project due. Don't tell your spouse.

29. Take up stock car racing. It's America's number-one spectator sport. Did you know that?

30. Buy a pickup truck, a shotgun and cowboy boots. Learn to say, "There ya go!"

31. Take up racquetball and take out your frustrations on a poor little ball.

32. Drive across the United States and back without stopping for anything except pit stops. See if your spouse misses you.

33. Walk around the house nude. See if your spouse notices you.

34. Learn to play the guitar, harmonica and bass drum at the same time while singing.

35. Take up the trumpet in the same room as the computer.

36. See how fat you can get on peanut butter and jelly. That will teach your spouse … if your spouse notices.

37. Get a sex-change operation. Get another operation to change it back.

38. Reorganize your spouse's computer desk … daily.

39. Take up gardening … with a chainsaw.

40. Write a romance novel. Write two.

41. Go to Disneyland.

42. Add a new room to the house with no electrical outlets. This will keep the computers out.

43. Go to Europe for three months.

44. Hire a voodoo witch to haunt the computer.

45. Start a new religious cult and make all the members give you all their money.

46. Become a nude model for a computer magazine. Maybe your spouse will notice you then.

47. Brew beer in the garage. Drink it all yourself.

48. Feed your spouse a new dish every night. Leave out one of the ingredients.

49. Wear combat boots to bed. That's all.

50. Organize a local chapter of Computer Widow/Widowers of American (CWWA). See Chapter 10, 11 or whatever it is.

Some of these ideas are admittedly cruel and certainly not all of them are for you. But there is such a variety here, and the ideas are so diverse, that you are bound to find one or two that will really turn you on.

If reading this list does not spark even a tiny little bit of inspiration for you, then you should arrange you own funeral, for you are most certainly brain-dead. Who could blame your spouse for falling in love with a machine? We suggest you get off your butt and do something.

CHAPTER 7

Amusement for the Computer Widow/Widower

Computers are a world unto themselves: they have their own language, equipment, way of life and way of thinking. It's often a strange way of thinking, leading computer addicts to frequently mystify and baffle their spouses. We'd like to help change this.

At Computer Publishing Enterprises, we have made it our mission in life to present the *human* side of computing. Often, this necessitates presenting the *humorous* side of computing. (Trust us—there is one.)

On the pages that follow is our treasured collection of computer jokes. If you read them fifty or sixty times you'll begin to get a glimpse into your computer-addicted spouse's techno sense of humor. Study them to get a better understanding of your spouse, or use them as a new means of interaction and communication with him or her. If your beloved has been locked in the computer room for days and doesn't respond to your plaintive cries for attention, break in and start reciting these jokes. They just might be the key to reaching a new level of understanding and affinity with your spouse.

And if that doesn't work, we've also included three fun-filled, challenging crossword puzzles. We feel these to be an excellent source of entertainment and amusement for all those hours you spend alone. They're also rather educational—a good way to drill yourself on understanding and pronouncing all those computer techno-terms. Enjoy!

COMPUTER WIDOW/WIDOWER JOKES

- How come grown men can stay up all night programming a computer, but can't take five minutes to do any housework?

- Many men prefer to spend time with their computers over a woman. And they call dogs a dumb animal.

- It's no wonder computer hackers have such a bad image. After all, how much can you have in common with someone who thinks Star Trek is the height of American culture?

- Computers have helped my husband and me discover a birth control method that's 100 percent effective. We call it abstinence.

- Women, can't live with them, can't live without them. Is that why so many people get married instead?

- If we only use 10 percent of our brain, that means we're using 90 percent ignorance to choose our next date.

- People like Macintosh computers because they use icons instead of words to get their message across. Now wasn't that the whole purpose of literacy in the first place?

- My wife threatened that if I don't spend more time with her and less time with my computer, she's going to leave me. So I got her a modem so she could still keep in touch.

- My husband just bought two more megabytes of memory, and yet he still can't remember our anniversary.

- Wife: "Computers aren't so bad. Now I can spend as much money as I want and modify the spreadsheet so my husband never knows."

"Lately you've been so much easier to talk to in the morning."

- Speaking in computer terms, our marriage is overdue for an upgrade, needs better documentation, but is already full of bugs.

- Why do women bother wearing fancy dresses, perfumes, and jewelry? The quickest way to get a man's attention is to unplug his computer before he can save three hours worth of work.

- To computers, people are totally illogical. Although two people can speak the same language, how come they still can't understand each other?

- How come a man can program a $5,000 IBM computer, but can't figure out how to set the time on a VCR?

- Q) What kind of macro should Lotus program into their next spreadsheet?
  A) One that will make your spouse stand up, turn off the computer, put away the potato chips, and wash the dishes.

- Q) When are you most likely to hear the word "modem"?
  A) When your spouse hands you the potato chips and says, "Get me some modem things."

- Q) What's a serial port?
  A) Red wine poured over your grape nuts.

- Q) What's multi-tasking?
  A) Typing with one hand and reaching for the potato chips with the other.

- Q) Why did the man put wheels on his computer and push it toward the wall?
  A) He wanted to "back up" his hard drive.

- Q) What's the best way to use a "home floor plan" program?
  A) You run the program to see where the furniture fits best; your spouse moves the furniture.

- Q) What should you do if you finally find a program that will do half your work for you?
  A) Buy two.

- Q) What's the longest minute in the day?
  A) When your spouse calls in from the computer room, "Honey, I'll be there in just a minute."

- Q) What's a computer hacker?
  A) Somebody who gets distracted by a program and swallows a potato chip the wrong way.

- Q) What *don't* you want to do when your child brings home a disk containing his very first computer program?
  A) Stick it on the refrigerator with a magnet so everybody can admire it.

- Q) What animals *didn't* enter Noah's ark in pairs?
  A) Bugs. They came in software.

- Q) What did one computer nerd say to the other?
  A) I can't tell; they all talk in numbers.

- Mavis the wealthy computer widow drove up in a fine limousine to where her friends were standing. Stopping to chat awhile, she had the chauffeur open the door. After enjoying a few juicy bits of gossip, the computer widow wriggled back into the limo, dripping with diamonds and oozing French perfume. "What's Mavis' secret?" asked one of the group. "Oh, she just made a deal with her husband the nerd. For every bite, she gets two-bits!"

"I'm beginning to worry about his relationship with that thing."

■ I belong to Computer Widows Anonymous. Whenever I feel like getting married, they send over a guy in a T-Shirt eating potato chips who sits in front of my T.V.'s monitor and ignores me.

■ Q) What did the geography teacher say to the student?
 A) Where is San Diego, Carmen?

■ Starry-eyed girl to friend: "Ohh, I just met the cutest guy, and he's an expert in sexual yoga, too!
 "Oh yeah?" drawled her cynical girlfriend. "What makes you say that?"
 "He said he could spreadsheet in Lotus, quicker than *1-2-3!*

■ Why did the programmer buy a laptop and a yacht?
 He wanted to program in sea!

■ A programmer explaining assembly language to his mom brings new meaning to the word "mother bored."

■ Q) What did the two programmers say to each other after meeting at a seminar?
 A) Have your modem call my modem, and we'll do data.

■ College coed: "My computer dating service came up with a perfect gentleman for me."
 Girlfriend: "Then why do you look so glum?"
 College coed: "You're right; I should cheer up. After all, I still have another three goes."

■ A programmer walked into a bar with his laptop. Ordering a beer, he said to the bartender, "Hey, I'll bet you ten bucks this computer can talk."
 "You're on," said the bartender, whipping a ten from behind the counter.
 Turning to the laptop, the programmer said, "What's the name of a beetle that can flip to his feet when you put him on his back?"
 "Click," responded the computer.

The bartender scratched his head, and said he'd double the bet if the computer answered the next question correctly.

"All right," the programmer said. Turning to the computer, he said, "What's the nickname of an astronaut named 'Aldrin'?"

"Buzz," said the computer.

Catching on, the bartender said, "All right, wise guy. Let me try. Fifty bucks says he can't do it again."

The bartender turned to the computer and said, "Who starred in the movie *Rocky*?"

The laptop replied, "Sylvester Stallone."

The programmer winked, took his money, and left.

- One waif was talking to another.

  "Yeah, I finally had to run away from home," the boy sighed.

  "Things were getting pretty bad, eh?" his ragged companion queried.

  "You said it. First they fired my dad at his work. It seems they found a computer that could do everything dad did, and more," the boy explained.

  "That's not so bad," growled his friend.

  "It gets worse," the first boy countered. "Yesterday, my mom ran out and bought one."

- Brother to sister: "It sounds like Dad's losing at *Fire of the Dungeons and Dragons* again."

  Sister: "Oh, he's trying to play a computer game?"

  Brother: "No, he's trying to sneak into bed after staying up all night on the computer."

- Q) How many programmers does it take to change a light bulb?

  A) None. It's a hardware problem.

- Q) What's the difference between a food processor and a computer processor?
  A) After using a food processor, you have something to show for your efforts.

- Q) Why did the programmer have an attitude problem?
  A) He had a chip on his shoulder.

- Q) What's a nerd's favorite seven-course meal?
  A) A bag of Doritos and a six-pack of Jolt Cola.

"This policy offers double indemnity for computer widows!"

COMPUTER WIDOW/WIDOWER
CROSSWORD PUZZLES

You may know more about computers than you thought. These puzzles were designed to bring out your hidden computer knowledge by tapping into your general knowledge in other areas.

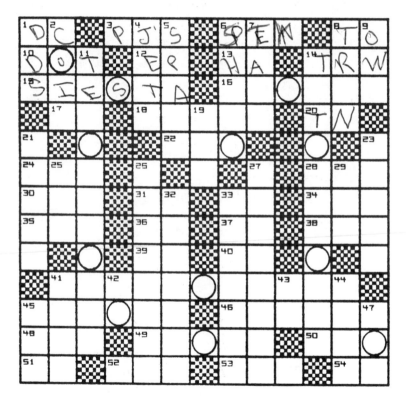

Rearrange the circled letters to complete the answer to the following question:

Why Did the Teenage Mutant Ninja Turtles Cross the Road?

To Get to the

— — — — —   — — — — — —

ACROSS CLUES

1. U.S. capital.
3. Nightwear.
6. Pig abode.
8. For.
10. Polka ___ .

12. Orlando's future city: ___COT.
13. Exclamation.
14. They use computers to track your credit history.
15. Afternoon nap.
16. Choice.
17. Southern state.
18. Video game comparison.
20. Nashville state.
22. Consume.
24. Every (Latin, abbr.).
28. "Let the buyer b___re."
30. 7 (Latin).
31. Input/Output (abbr.).
33. Boulder state.
34. Comedian.
35. At the end of company names.
36. Commercial.
37. I exist (abbr.).
38. Iron.
39. Langley (abbr.).
40. Food instructions (abbr.).
41. These might be Mork's time units.
45. This would take forever without computers.
46. They used to be in movie theaters.
48. Hawkeye and B.J.
49. Magical spirit.
50. Communications company.
51. Padres' town (abbr.).
52. Typewriter part.
53. Attempt.
54. He wrote *War of the Worlds*.

DOWN CLUES

1. Dentist letters.
2. Nickel.
4. *Top Gun* had computers in these.
5. Hal was the computer in this movie (with 32 down).
6. A robot came to life in this movie (with 33 down).
7. It stores information or music.
8. Disney computer movie.
9. Possess.
11. They fix computers.
14. The champion.
19. Tree.
21. The letter in the middle of the puzzle stands for this.
23. See 29 down.
25. Time measurement (abbr.).
26. Talking part of a script.
27. Music writer.
29. A computer almost starts WW III in this movie (with 23 down).
32. See 5 down.
33. See 6 down.
41. Heavy computer user.
42. *The Hunt for Red October* has one of these (abbr.).
43. New England state.
44. Look for (abbr.).
45. They store music (abbr.).
47. Droop.

Rearrange the circled letters to complete the answer to the following question:

Why Did the Thirsty Astronaut Go to the Keyboard?

Because He Heard it Had a

— — — —   — — —

ACROSS CLUES

1. Electrical measurement.
3. StreetHawk had a computerized one.
7. Quayle.
9. He had a computer in his cave (with 11 across).
11. See 9 across.
12. Received.
13. Steal.
15. Happy.
16. Android from 22 down.
18. ___head.

19. Summer time in the Rockies.
22. Subject-Verb-Object (abbr.).
24. Third letter.
25. Expletive from 9 across.
26. ___ Maria.
27. Ballplayer Mel ___.
28. Wire service.
29. Is transmitted.
31. 3.14 . . . .
32. ____vision.
33. This show had a computerized car: Knight _____.
35. Our star.

36. I in CIA (abbr.).
38. Baseball referee.
40. Some horror shows give you a lot of this.
42. The "Y."
43. Maxwell Smart talked to him in the cone of silence.
44. The first computers?
46. Extra period.
47. Australian animal.
48. Goes with joy, able and counter.

DOWN CLUES

1. Kilobyte (abbr.).
2. Toasty.
4. Computerized timers time these events; Ol__pics.
5. The computers in the Outer Limits sometimes looked like they were made out of this.
6. Type of road (abbr.).
7. The submarine in this show had a huge computer; "_____ _o the Bottom of the Sea."
8. CA Time.
10. Thumb or Swift.

12. MacGyver uses them to get out of jams.
14. Mr. T on "The A-Team."
15. _____-Roman.
16. _____ Chronicles.
17. Mork ___ _____.
20. Just say "no" to this.
21. Perhaps the first TV show to have computers: "_____ Zone."
22. The ship's computer wasn't smarter than Spock on this show.
23. Eight (Roman).
30. Direction.
31. Stinky.
34. Dance.
35. This show had a robot with a personality: "Lost __ _____" (with 45 down).
37. "Yes you did!" "__ _ didn't!"
39. Record company.
41. Earnings from operations (abbr.).
42. You (Southern variation).
43. Business (abbr.).
45. With 35 down.

Here's a puzzle you and your spouse can work on together. There are a set of clues for the non computer-literate and another set of clues for the computer user. Have fun!

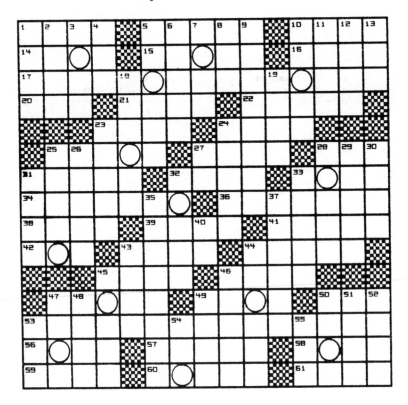

Rearrange the circled letters to complete the saying.

When in Doubt

_ _ _ _ _ The _ _ _ _ _ _ _

COMPUTER CLUES

ACROSS CLUES

1. Power Units.
5. Discards unneeded data.
10. Binary is ___ 2.
14. Fibbed.
15. Added RAM can give your computer more of this.
16. Egg-shaped.
17. Computer date?
20. ___work.
21. File condition.
22. Grasses.

23. Evils.
24. Computers can help it think faster.
25. Proa.
27. ____ware.
28. Millions of watts (abbr.).
31. Someone who puts information on a disk.
32. Hard disk test: Comp____.
33. Goes with chain or wheel: ____y.
34. Finishes.
36. Gives a value to a variable.
38. I in CAI.
39. Stud.
41. Most input devices require these.
42. Language used to describe a language: ___alanguage.
43. The bank has a computerized record of this.
44. Type of circuit that stops the delivery of a signal for a specified time.
45. Winglike structure.
46. The Source charges these.
47. Summarize.
49. Stop a Program.
50. CAD/___.
53. Computerized introduction service?
56. All.
57. Bird.
58. Selection within a menu.
59. Academic admissions test (abbr.).
60. _____ III.
61. Salamander.

DOWN CLUES

1. ____ Kay.
2. Input devices.
3. Vegetable fuel.
4. Synchronous data link control: ___C.
5. Systems interaction.
6. They're in the middle of floppies.
7. Arab country.
8. Rain (abbr.).
9. Computer crime can lead to meeting these people.
10. A good program can keep you from getting this.
11. A hacker is an ____ computer user.
12. "Don't give me any of your ____."
13. Deer.
18. VGA has 256 of these.
19. Notch.
23. Just because someone doesn't use computers doesn't mean they are this.
24. Sometimes you need to make this type of decision when copying software.
25. Meat, in Spain.
26. "_____ ye lubbers!"
27. Russia (abbr.).
28. _____ Carta.
29. Gusty.
30. Noisy hard drive sound.
31. Undesirable movement of an image on a monitor.
32. Blank character.
33. A modem does it.
35. Not covered.
37. Spread_____.
40. Sperry's "AT" model.
43. Axillary.
44. Ctrl-Alt-_____.
45. What you do to a test when you really know the information.
46. A cube has six.
47. Memory types.
48. Stove.
49. Hebrew dance.
50. Allege.
51. Afresh.
52. M in MIS.
53. Operating system.
54. Monitor type.
55. ___gle-sided disk.

NON-COMPUTER CLUES

ACROSS CLUES

1. Electrical Units.
5. Lamb steaks.
10. ____ball.
14. Deceived.
15. Vitality.
16. Egg-like.
17. Computer date?
20. Hair ____.
21. Unclose.
22. Woodwinds.
23. Sicknesses.
24. Brain.
25. Boat.
27. Fluffy.
28. Those most worthy (abbr.).
31. Rescuer.
32. Ride the waves.
33. Podium.
34. He does it to a present (2 wds.).
36. Appoints.
38. Immediately (abbr.).
39. Finger ____.
41. Arm enders.
42. Greeted.
43. Bank file (abbr.).
44. Hold back.
45. Winglike structure.
46. Dues.
47. Review.
49. Stop..
50. __corder.
53. Computerized introduction
    service?
56. Science magazine.
57. Heron.
58. Article.
59. Academic admissions test (abbr.).
60. It might be after cBASE?
61. Eye of ____.

DOWN CLUES

1. Alda or King.
2. Pixie and Dixie.
3. ____ moss.
4. Horse riding seat (abbr.).
5. Duo.
6. Openings.
7. Arab country.
8. Rain (abbr.).
9. Law officers.
10. What you might become while
    your spouse is computing.
11. Eager.
12. Impudent speech.
13. Large deer.
18. Hues.
19. Depression.
23. Just because someone doesn't
    use computers doesn't mean they
    are this.
24. Ethical.
25. ____ Asada.
26. "____ ye lubbers!"
27. Under, in Paris.
28. ____ Carta.
29. Chicago weather.
30. Snake sound.
31. Fish do it.
32. The final frontier.
33. Uses a telephone.
35. Not covered.
37. Bedding.
40. Pronoun.
43. Axillary.
44. Erase.
45. What you do to a test if you
    study hard.
46. Fronts.
47. LA ballplayers.
48. Stove.
49. Hebrew dance.
50. Quote.
51. Afresh.
52. Bosses (abbr.).
53. Two, in Mexico.
54. Red-Green-Blue (abbr.).
55. Transgress.

The answers to these crossword puzzles can be found at the back of the book in Appendix B, starting on page 145.

CHAPTER 8

*The Computer Widow's Guide
to Computers
By Linda Williams*

Yeah, okay, so I don't like it any more than you, but it has him sitting there all day and night driving me crazy. So I decide that I'm going to find out what this thing is all about.

Well, he talks about it in all kinds of technogobble and I can't understand a word of it from here to there. Okay? So one day while I'm down at the mall watching a lady with three screaming kids driving her up a wall, I say to myself, "It's time to fight back and learn what's going on. How can I fight something I can't understand?"

My girlfriends are always telling me that I should really get to understand the contraption if I want to be able to fight back. It's sort of like pretending to like football games on television and everything. I mean, I don't mind going to football games—there's the tailgating before and all. And at the games you can see all the funny looking people and the way they dress. And the girls at the games are really going all out to impress, usually without much success. That's kind of fun, but the games themselves? Come on! I've never seen anything so silly in all my life.

So, anyway, I'm going to understand how the thing works, right? I go down to the book store and look for a book on computers, but they all seem to have too many pages. Are you kidding me? Six hundred pages? Come on!

Maybe I should talk to my friend Cathy. She's the one who is a little bit into computers. She writes letters for work and stuff like that. She has lots of time for that since her boyfriend took off. You know, he just split one day without even so much as a word. She was bummed at first, but after a while she decided that he was a jerk anyway. I always wanted to tell her that.

Well, I say to Cathy that if I'm ever going to get a communication thing going with my lump of a husband I need to know a little bit more about computers. I need some words to get his attention.

So Cathy's great. She tells me how the thing works and for the first time I actually understand it. It's so simple I couldn't believe it. Cathy says that they made up all those fancy words just to confuse regular people. It sure worked on me.

What I can't understand is why this computer has to take up so much space. It's not like we have a big mansion or something. All this stuff uses up more space than I do! At first it was just this little box on the desk in the corner. But there was no place for a printer. I told him that if you could see what you were doing on the TV screen, why did you need a printer? Besides, when it runs, it's noisy and interferes with the TV.

You should have seen the dustballs building up behind it. I wouldn't even go near it. One time while he was adding some new gadget on it, he blew a fuse or something—right while I was watching a tape of my show. Total darkness! Can you believe it? Now besides the dustballs, there's these long plug-in things called power bars and wires all over the place.

Cathy says that a computer is kind of like a VCR. It's just a video tape machine with a television. Well, sort of. You can watch shows and stuff, only they don't have my show, which is on at two o'clock every day. At work they're real rude and won't let me watch my show, so I videotape it and never miss a one. Well, I did forget to set the machine one day. I was really bummed. I know how the VCR works and Cathy tells me that a computer is like a VCR, sort of.

I say, "Those flippy disks are really like cassette tapes?" And Cathy says, "Yeah, only they're smashed out flat with a hammer like a CD or a record. But they're made out of the same stuff as a video cassette." She goes on to tell me that they are really called "floppy disks."

Well, if you ask me, I think that's a pretty stupid name, because, besides the rude connotations, the things aren't floppy at all. The big ones might be called flexies, but the little ones should be called stiffies. Cathy says that they are all called "floppies."

So I say to Cathy, "You mean the computer show is kept on one of those floppies?" And she says, "Yeah, and they're also kept on the hard disk."

Well, my ears perked up at this. I'd heard my one-and-only mumble something about a hard disk at breakfast one morning. I didn't say anything, but I remember it real well, because he was in a real bad mood. He had been computing all night while I was changing stations in the bedroom. Suddenly, there he was standing at the door. It was only midnight and there he was.

At first I thought that something good might happen, but then I could see he was in a bad mood. I knew it was too good to be true. He's about as romantic as a slug. Before we were married we used to go to the movies and stuff. Now, he works the computer and I work the VCR.

Well, anyway, he's kind of steaming. Not out loud, but under his breath. I know that something's happened to his own true love. I think great, now maybe I'll see more of him. No such luck; he's worse than ever. The next morning he's muttering something about a stupid hard disk and I can't agree more. He's had a hard disk crash.

Cathy says that a hard disk crash is a real bummer. I ask if it's worse than a stiffie disk crash and she says it is far worse. She says that a hard disk can hold a ton more shows than a stiffie. It is sort of like having a whole year of "my two o'clock show" on one tape. Can you imagine that? A whole year? "It would take forever to re-wind it," I tell Cathy.

Cathy tells me that you don't have to re-wind the hard disk or the stiffies; they are more like CDs in that way. So, that morning my ever-so-dear hubby offers to show me the problem with the hard disk. Now I'm trapped. I can't even roll my eyes because he's actually looking at me. I say to myself that I hope this doesn't take as long as a football game and I say to him, "I'd love to, Honey."

He takes me over to the computer and points to the box. On the TV it's saying, "FAT allocation error" or something like that. Now I remember this because a lot of my girlfriends have this problem. Not me, of course, because I do my Jazzercise two mornings a week before going to work. I have to get up early to do it, but it's worth it because you don't have so many geeks trying to hit on you at that time. I think geeks have trouble getting up that early or it takes them too long to put on their geek face.

The afternoons are geek-time at my fitness place. They come out in herds. Of course most of the afternoon women are geeks with their dimpled thighs making their mating calls while pretending to get a workout.

So, anyway, I say "Where's the hard disk?" and he points to a little light on the computer. Now, this blows me away. How can a little light be the cause of all his problems? Of course I don't say anything then, but Cathy tells me that the hard disk is actually inside most computers and you can't see it at all. The light just tells you when it is on.

"So how do you change the tape to put on a new show?" I ask.

Cathy says that you don't; you just copy from the stiffie to the hard disk, just as if you had two VCRs. That's why computers are so expensive. They have two, or more, VCRs. She says that stiffies won't hold as many shows as the hard disk.

I ask Cathy "What's software?" Now, this will blow you away. Software is the shows. Can you believe it? It's so simple. They have to make up a dumb word like software to talk about their computer shows. Can you imagine what people would say to me if I said something like, "Let's check the *TV Guide* and see what software is on tonight." But Cathy says that's all there is to it.

I ask Cathy why the nerds try to make everything so difficult to understand. But Cathy is the understanding type and says that they don't even know that they're nerds and it's just the way that they think. She says that they would name their kids after numbers if you would let them. Even on the football field they replace the names with numbers. It's the only way you can tell them apart ... (like you would want to, always scratching themselves and spitting).

So, anyway, software is the shows. Okay, so that morning, my sweeter-than-sweet says to me, "Every time I reboot I get this FAT allocation error," or something like that.

I say, "Not in my house you don't!" So, later, Cathy tells me that reboot means to get the computer going again. Like when they say that "the damn thing" has crashed again and won't do anything. It's frozen staring off into space. Just think, a machine staring off into space. Well, that's when you have to reboot the computer.

Cathy says that when you turn the computer on, "it boots up." Then if it crashes, which is popular with computers, you have to reboot it. She says that rebooting is like what she used to have to do late at night with her jerk boyfriend after the first time that night. I can't believe it. I can't even get my lump of man to boot, much less reboot.

Cathy tells me that when a computer boots or reboots it's kind of like putting Dick Clark inside the computer. You see Dick is playing the tunes and running the shows and he has to be there for us to see anything. Now, I don't much like Dick Clark, so Cathy says that it's also like Sonny and Cher reruns, you know before they broke up. She says that it doesn't matter who is inside as long as there is someone running the show.

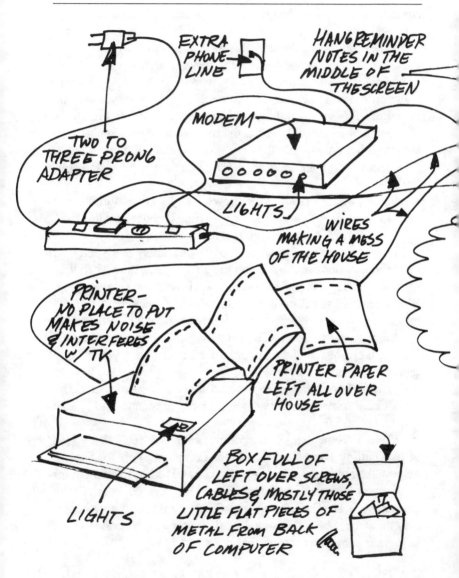

Use this life-like rendering as a guide to the techno-clutter which has invaded your home.

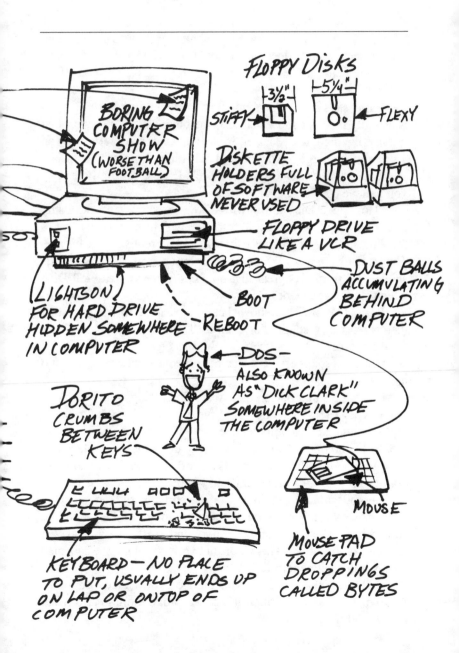

Cathy says that the host for the computer show is called DOS. (She pronounced it "doss" as in Hoss Cartwright.) Now, if I had a kid, I sure wouldn't call the child DOS. Of course, who can afford kids?

Cathy says that DOS stands for Disk Operating System, but it is actually the host show that runs the other shows. She says that it's like having Dick Clark or Sonny and Cher run every show on TV. I almost gagged. No wonder I don't like computers. So when you boot or reboot a computer, there's Dick Clark in there. Can you believe it?

"How does Dick know what shows to show?" I ask. Cathy goes on to say that you get to tell Dick which shows you want to see. I mean some of the music that Dick plays really shows his age. They must have a coffin out back for him just in case it's his last show. So I think it's great that on a computer you can tell Dick which shows you want to see.

I want to know what shows I can watch and Cathy tells me that there aren't any soaps, not even a "Dallas" or "Dynasty." So, what's the use? If these people who make computers would get smart and put soaps on them, maybe someone besides nerds would use them.

Cathy says that one show is word processing, which is like a fancy typewriter. I see enough of typewriters all day long, thank you very much. The computer does have a keyboard and it actually looks like the ones at work. The letters are in the same place and everything! Only there's no nerds at work, and nerds leave Dorito crumbs all over the computer desk. I know.

Another thing it can do is database software, which is like an address book, only it's hard to carry it with you. Then there are spreadsheets, that's mostly numbers and stuff. "Come on, get real!" I say to Cathy. "This whole network is going to be canceled if they don't get better programming."

Cathy says that's exactly what the shows are called: programs. And when a show is written it's called programming. "So, what else would it be?" I say.

I knew that the hero-of-my-dreams did programming, because he would call it that. When he was programming, he would go into a coma which involved only him and the computer. (I once wandered around the house naked for two hours while he was in this state. He never noticed.) He would only occasionally snap out of it long enough to show me some unintelligible words printed on that long paper with the little holes on the side that he leaves all over the place and beam, "Look what I did!"

Of course, I would pat him on the head and say, "Isn't that special?" Ignoring my lack of enthusiasm, he would then explain in detail what he had accomplished. Naturally, I would nod approvingly until he would wander back to his computer. When I really want to ask him a question, I just put one of those little sticky notes right on his computer TV screen. After he gets one of those crashes, he gets back to me.

Cathy says that there are some programs that are games, but they're for kids. Yeah, my hubby is one of those kids. He has even decided that his computer needs to talk to other computers. You see, these nerds have even figured out how to make computer telephones. They're called modems. Now we have two phone lines. I can think of a lot of other things I'd rather have two of.

And there was this one day that the light-of-my-life came home and said that he just bought a mouse. Just what I needed, a rodent to clean up after. Then he showed me that it was a toy mouse attached to the computer. Just what I needed, a rodent to clean up after. When he moved the mouse around, a little arrow would move on the screen and point to things. Just what I needed, a rodent to clean up after. It seemed pretty stupid to me. You would need three hands to use the computer: two for the keyboard and one for the mouse. Maybe this is something to do with a friend.

Then he added a joystick. Now, he needed four hands. Next he wants a lightpen so he can point directly to the screen. Come on . . . it would take five hands, which is at least three people—and I'm not having that many nerds in my house at one time.

Cathy started to tell me about laser printers, but I said that I had had enough. If I learned any more my brain was going to explode. Besides, there was a sale at Nordstrom's and they would be expecting us. Before we left, I looked in on my sweet, adorable hubby, who was glued to the computer screen as if it were one of his football games, without the cheering, and shook my head.

If only they had soaps.

"You nagged me for twenty years about reading the newspaper at the table. So I quit!"

CHAPTER 9

Dear Digital Dave

Dear Digital Dave,
My husband and I recently bought a computer. I say we bought it, but I don't know anything about computers, so my husband does all the computing. The problem is, he computes all the time.

He has tried to teach me BASIC, but I don't understand an IF/THEN from a GOTO. I'm feeling left out, and I don't want to waste his time if I'm not really going to understand it. Do you have a suggestion on how to participate in computing? I just feel so dumb when I try to keep up with my husband.

Please withhold my name because I'd die of embarrassment if my husband knew I wrote you (on a typewriter) this letter.

Mrs. X

Dear Mrs. X,
I'll bet hundreds of husbands will think this letter was written by their wives, because they know they are guilty of hogging the brand-new computer. My wife had to tell off a neighbor who was monopolizing their new AT while the kids had to use the old Apple II clone. His wife insists on using the old Apple, so sometimes it works in reverse.

Anyway, on to your problem. You need to have your hubby get you started using the computer to do something. Learning BASIC is an easy way to get a handle on programming a computer, but most people don't write programs, they use the computer for something.

For instance, you typed your letter on a typewriter. Yuk! Have him show you how to use a word processor program. You only need to learn a few commands, like how to load and to save a file, before you are more productive than a typewriter ever was. Just having a backspace key to fix oopses is a big step forward. Later you can learn how to do the fancy formatting and automatic indexing.

Are you the secretary of your PTA? Keeping track of the membership roll is a hassle, isn't it? Have your computer jock set up a database file to help you out. Let him do all the up-front setup stuff, then you type in all the names and addresses.

Let him do the sorting and printing the first few times, then you work your way in. Pretty soon you will find yourself a database expert, and you can set up your own recipe file, or keep track of the family CD collection.

Digital Dave

Dear Digital Dave,

I am a computer widow in the true sense of the word. My husband is no longer too enamored of a computer to pay attention to me. You see, he's gone to that bit bucket in the sky.

I know it sounds strange for a 67-year-old widow to use language like that, but my late husband was a programmer from the early days of punched cards. He always worked on the mainframe computers and never took up with the personal computers that are all the rage today.

Since my husband worked with computers all day, we never had a computer in the house, and I never really learned much about them. Here is the reason I am writing to you; I have a lot more time on my hands since I retired and my husband passed away, so I have become much more involved in my church and their good works.

The deacons at the church wanted to ease the paperwork load on the volunteer workers, so they went out and bought an IBM PS-2 model 80 personal computer to help out. Problem is, nobody knows what to do with it.

Most of the people active in the church are either retired or housewives. Where can we get help?

Muriel Harris

Dear Muriel,

I should be so lucky. An IBM PS-2 model 80 is no light-duty machine. It should be able to handle any computing tasks you and the other church members can throw at it.

Anyway, I can see three main areas of use for your computer. One would be to keep account of the church's finances. The second function might be to organize your membership lists and aid you asking for donations without duplication. Third, the computer could help you to replace the minister's expensive transcriptionist with a low-cost volunteer. It's amazing how a backspace key can improve the performance of even a hunt-and-pecker over someone with a typewriter.

How do you go about getting the help you need to get started on these three areas? The church finances should be handled by a program that is designed just for church finances. The best place for help in this area is other churches. Call other churches and find out how they handle the coin of the realm.

Membership lists for the largest church can be handled by even the simplest database programs. A computer user's group would be the best place to get help on setting up your files.

Check out your local computer publication for the date and time of meetings of group with names like dBASErs Beginner's Group, or anything with "database" or "dBASE" in it. Then go to some meetings and don't be afraid to ask questions and get some help.

Word processing is pretty much a sit-down session with the tutorial that comes with the word processor. Just try the basic commands and hack through it. In an hour you and your computer should be able to do anything a typewriter can do.

In a week or two, the desktop publishing capabilities of a high-end (read: expensive) word processor like WordPerfect *or* Microsoft Word *will have you cranking out the Sunday bulletin in no time (and a lot better looking than what that old IBM Selectric could do). Of course, having one of those fancy laser printer would help.*

Digital Dave

Dear Digital Dave,

I've read your column for years, even though I am not a "power user." I use my computer, or should I say, I used to use my computer for simple word processing such as letter writing and a form letter at Christmas for all the family.

It was nice to have a piece of machinery that would be available any time to do my bidding, at least until my son took interest in the computer. You see, I am a single mom with a 14-year-old son.

We used to take walks to the park after I got home from work, or go on picnics on the weekends, but no more. Since he discovered all the games that are available for my PC, I can't get him off of it. Not only does he not want to spend time with me, he won't let me use my computer.

What can I do? I can't afford to buy him his own computer, and he's the only man in my life. I'm feeling lonely!

Jane Brown

Dear Jane,

Don't worry. In a year or so he'll discover girls. He still won't want to spend time with you, but at least you can have your computer back.

I'm not an authority on interpersonal relationships, other than the fact that I have a few, but I think there is a bit of selfishness on your part. First you talk about sharing time with your son, then you talk about "your" computer.

He has to grow up, and he needs relationships with others. I would encourage him to get out and get involved in some activities with people his own age, and other adults for that matter.

How about some compromises? He likes computers; take him to a computer users group meeting where he can learn more about computers, meet other people, and still spend some time with you. How about learning some of those games and give him someone to play against?

Digital Dave

Dear Digital Dave,

Usually a computer widow is a forgotten wife whose husband buys a computer and disappears into the den every night instead of spending time with her. I'm just the opposite: my wife works with computers all day, then when she gets home she's too tired to do anything. I usually end up cooking and eating my dinner alone.

How can working with a computer wear one out so? All she does is sit there all day and stare at the screen and press keys. Is there anything I can do to reinvigorate her?

Henry Hamilton

Dear Henry,

How about meeting her at the door after work wrapped in Saran Wrap, and nothing else? Oh, I think somebody else already suggested that.

This isn't the place to tell you how to get her interested in things other than computers, but maybe I can help you with ideas of how to reduce the stress of working with a computer.

First, she could use some exercise. How and where you induce her to do some exercise I'll leave to you. When working with a computer, she should get up out of the chair and stretch at least once per hour. It's amazing how a computer problem that you've been working on suddenly goes away after a brief break to get the blood moving to the brain again.

Eye strain is another computer-related problem, causing headaches and the urge to crawl into bed and pull the covers over your head. The strain on the old peepers can be tamed by arranging the lighting to reduce glare on the screen, adjusting the brightness and contrast to a comfortable level, which might require that the room lights be dimmed a bit, and cleaning the screen.

I find I need to clean the screen in my office about once a day to keep the dust off. Of course the road construction out in front of the plant where I work probably makes it worse than usual.

Last but not least, get comfortable. I went to Price Club and bought myself a high-backed leather office chair for $199. I can sit back and pound the keyboard all night in comfort. It's amazing how many people sit on an uncomfortable chair all day at work, then can't figure out why they are beat at the end of the day.

Also, putting the keyboard on her lap will take a lot of strain off her shoulders and upper back. Trying to hold her little arms up all day to type with a keyboard on top of a desk would be more work than laying bricks.

I hope some of these suggestions will help her though her day with a bit (or maybe a byte) left over for you in the evening.

Digital Dave

Dear Digital Dave,

My husband used to watch sports on the TV all the time. Now he has a home computer and he stays up late every night. How can I get him to pay attention to me and come to bed early?

Computer Widow

Dear Widow,

I don't know. I'm sitting in front of my computer at 3 a.m. writing this column. If you find a way, tell my wife. I could use some sleep.

Digital Dave

"And now ... she is accusing me of spending more time with you than I spend with her."

CHAPTER 10

Computer Widows/Widowers of America

It has been commonly recognized that a computer entering the home is not unlike the death of the spouse who brings the machine into the home.

Ergo, the world is now becoming encumbered with computer widow/widowers. The loneliness and rejection experienced by the bereaved spouse is not commonly understood and little recognized. The time has come for Computer Widows/Widowers of American (CWWA). Surviving spouses can now band together and commiserate over their shared turmoil.

CWWA is dedicated to the aid and entertainment of computer abused spouses everywhere. After all, they are the ones who are left to do all the real work, while their spouses fool around with those blasted machines. It is planned that CWWA will have a newsletter chock-full of ideas and entertainment for CWWA members.

Support groups will be formed throughout America to counsel and console fellow widows/widowers. These support groups will provide training and diversions, such as bowling and pinochle.

CWWA is in the formative stages right now, but once the CWWA is up and running, national conventions will take place regularly in exotic locales like Hawaii and Las Vegas. (Why not?)

If you would like more information about CWWA, or to give your ideas about what the CWWA should really do, please write to :

Computer Widow/Widowers of America
C/O Computer Publishing Enterprises
P.O. Box 23478
San Diego, CA 92123

We will respond within a reasonable period of time, or eat a bug.

APPENDICES

APPENDIX A

Glossary of Terms

APPLICATIONS SOFTWARE
This is software that does real things. It can be written in assembly language or a higher level language, but most users of applications software don't care which. All they see or care about is the end result. Some packages do business accounting, some sort addresses by name or zip code, others edit stories and still others check spelling. Applications software makes a computer a useful tool for almost anyone. (see software)

ASSEMBLY LANGUAGE
This is the lowest level computer language, as well as the fastest running language for a computer. Since it is written in the obscurity of hexadecimal code, it requires deep concentration and 16 fingers to program in assembly language. (see higher level languages)

BAUD RATE
Bits per second. The baud rate is the speed at which a computer can communicate with a device. Typical baud rates vary from 50 to 19,200. For modems, 300 and 1200 are common. The higher the baud rate the faster the computer can send and receive. Many problems are caused by having the computer set to a different baud rate from the device on-line. Most people operate at a baud rate much slower than their computer.

BIT

The smallest piece of computer information. Just as a "bit" of bread is the smallest piece one can eat. Unlike dropping a "bit" of bread, if you drop a computer "bit," you might lose the whole "loaf." (see byte, megabyte, gigabyte, K)

BUFFER

This is memory that is used as a corral for bits and bytes that are waiting to go somewhere. A printer with a baud rate slower than that of the computer can be more efficient by attaching a buffer. The computer dumps the data in the buffer and goes about other business while the printer grunts away at the task. A buffer's function is very similar to that of a child's playpen.

BULLETIN BOARD

This is a service, provided by a computer hooked up to a modem, with the ability to answer the telephone. It sits and waits for another computer to call, then answers the phone. It will send information it has stored to the other computer and receive whatever the other computer sends it. The function and use of the bulletin board depends on the person who programmed it.

BYTE

Eight bits. Everything in computers is measured in bytes. You can never have too many bytes. When shopping, always buy lots of bytes. (see megabyte, gigabyte, K)

DOT-MATRIX PRINTER

The printing head of this kind of printer is composed of rows and columns of tiny little hammers which strike the paper in a pattern determined by the computer to produce letters or numbers. The quality of output generally looks like what is considered a standard computer printout. The major advantages to the dot-matrix are speed and versatility. The versatility of the dot-matrix head not only allows all the required character sets, but also allows more than enough totally unintelligible characters through special programming. (see fully-formed character printer, laser printer)

E-PROM

Erasable Programmable Read Only Memory. Can only be erased with a special light in the back room behind the garage. (see PROM)

FLOPPY DISKETTES

Magnetic tape hammered out in the shape of a disk. Information is recorded magnetically on sectors and tracks on the disks. It is possible for the disk reading head to go directly to the sector where information is recorded without reading the entire disk. Much faster than the magnetic tape. (see magnetic tape)

FULLY FORMED CHARACTER PRINTER

Also known as a "Letter Quality" printer. (This refers to the quality of the letter's appearance, not the contents.) This kind of printer uses a daisy-wheel or thimble holding little spokes with each individual letter or number on a spoke. A hammer strikes the spoke against the paper, producing a character in much the same way as a typewriter. The printer is much faster than a typewriter and makes less typos. (see laser printer)

GIGABYTE

1,000 megabytes. There is an application for using this many bytes. It has something to do with the National Debt. (see K)

HARD DISK

Magnetic plates in hermetically-sealed boxes. Similar to floppy diskettes in operation, except they will hold about ten times as much information, are ten times faster and cost ten times the money. Comparing the use of magnetic tape, floppy diskettes and a hard disk is like comparing walking, a bicycle and a car. A person can certainly tell the difference and appreciate moving up to the next step, but it costs a little bit more each time.

HIGHER LEVEL LANGUAGES
These are computer languages which use more understandable, English-like words for code. COBOL, FORTRAN and BASIC are some examples of higher level languages. The commands are words like "GOTO," "DO WHILE" and "FOR NEXT." To write in these languages, a programmer must know where to tell the computer to "GOTO."

K
1,024 bytes. Some people believe a "K" is one thousand bytes. Not true! It is actually one thousand twenty-four bytes. Also known as a "KByte." (see megabyte and gigabyte)

LASER PRINTERS
Having less moving parts and using lasers, these things do beautiful work with exceptional speed. They also cost thousands and thousands of dollars, or more. Models with special laser security devices and death-rays are nice.

MAGNETIC TAPE
This is the same tape used with stereos. The computer information is stored magnetically on the tape. Large quantities of information can be stored on tape, making it good for backup of programs and data.

MASS STORAGE
A mechanical non-volatile memory device. Mass storage media includes paper tape, punch cards, magnetic tape, floppy diskettes and hard disks. Computer bits, bytes and stuff can be stored in large quantities on these mediums for later use by the computer. When the computer is turned off the information remains intact—barring physical damage by fire, theft or irate users.

MEGABYTE
1,000 KBytes. Oodles of bytes. Somewhere around a million, give or take a bit. (see gigabyte, K)

MODEM

MOdulator/DEModulator. This is a device that changes computer bits and bytes to sounds which can be sent over the telephone line to another modem which will change the sounds back into computer bits and bytes. The modem hooks up to the computer via an RS-232 port. The modem serves the same purpose for the computer as vocal cords do for a human being, only with much greater accuracy. (see bulletin board)

OFF-LINE

A device which is not hooked up to a computer. If a printer is off-line, it is not operating with the computer. A device can only be off-line if it has the capability of being on-line with the computer. Printers and modems can be off-line, but toasters and coffee pots can't. (see on-line)

ON-LINE

A device which is hooked up to a computer, enabling it to communicate directly with the central processing unit (CPU). In the on-line condition, the CPU sends bits and bytes to, and receives bits and bytes from, the device. Printers must be on-line to print. When a computer is used to communicate with databases via modem it is said to be on-line. (see bulletin board)

ON-LINE DATABASES

This is a huge computer with tons of data on its hard disks which can be accessed from a remote location via modem. It is very similar to a library, but it usually costs money to use it. It is faster than going to the library and saves the price of gas.

OUT OF LINE

Uncalled-for remarks about a person's computer, software or family.

PROM
Programmable Read Only Memory. This chip can only be programmed with a special gadget in the garage.

PAPER TAPE
Rolls of narrow paper with holes punched into it. The hole patterns represent computer information. It is very uncommon to see paper tape in conjunction with microcomputers. It is much more common to see paper tape in conjunction with parades.

PORT
This is a hole in the back of the computer. It is usually either a parallel port or a serial port. The parallel port sends all the bits in a byte out to the printer or other peripheral device in a row shoulder to shoulder, while a serial port sends all the bits out in a column one behind the other. A parallel port will send info faster, but certain devices such as modems use only serial ports. The most common serial port is the RS-232 port.

PRINTER
A mechanical device for typing out all the things the computer operator has created with the computer. It is generally considered a requirement for any serious computing. The printer is responsible for the recent rapid growth in the paper industry. One printer attached to a computer can single-handedly produce more paperwork than 150 bureaucrats working with pencils. (see dot-matrix printer, fully-formed character printer and laser printer)

PUNCH CARDS
Business-envelope sized cards with holes punched in them. The hole patterns are again the key to the computer information. They do not fit into floppy disk drives, therefore they are uncommon with the microcomputer. Mythology says that the huge mainframe computers use punch cards for snacks.

RAM

Random Access Memory. Temporary memory. The computer's working space where it puts everything being processed, manipulated, truncated, and masticated. The more RAM you have, the more information your computer can chew. However, if you lose power, you lose what's in RAM. There is also a stigma attached to having less than 64K Bytes of RAM.

ROM

Read Only Memory. Permanent memory. Also known as "Firmware." Similar to a library book. You can read it and use the information, but you are not allowed to write in it. ROM is often used to protect against one of the most serious threats to computing-operator error. (See PROM)

ROB

Read-Only Bed. The only activity taking place in the bed of a dedicated computer user, as observed by a spouse.

RANDOM ACCESS

Property of computer memory in which access time is independent of memory address; a technique for information management. Example: one places a piece of paper on his or her desk remembering the exact location. Later, the paper can be retrieved by going directly to the same location without handling every piece of paper on the desk. Known as the Random Access Desk (RAD). This system is easily destroyed in one pass by the Compulsive Desk Straightener (CDS).

SOFTWARE

Codes of bits and bytes stored in electro-magnetic media which tell the computer what to do and how to do it.

STONE

This is a popular mass storage medium in large bureaucratic organizations. It is generally used for policy and is chiseled in "stone."

The user-friendly computer

APPENDIX B

Crossword Puzzle Answers

WHY DID THE TEENAGE MUTANT
NINJA TURTLES CROSS THE ROAD?
TO GET TO THE

SHELL STATION

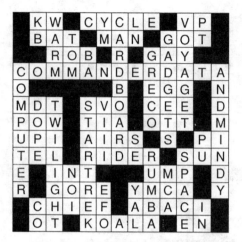

WHY DID THE THIRSTY ASTRONAUT
GO TO THE KEYBOARD?
BECAUSE HE HEARD IT HAD A

SPACE BAR

WHEN IN DOUBT
BLAME THE COMPUTER

Other computer books from
Computer Publishing Enterprises:

The Best FREE Time-Saving Utilities for the PC
By Wally Wang

101 Computer Business Ideas
By Wally Wang

DOS Secrets
By Dan Gookin

How to Get Started in Desktop Publishing
By the *ComputorEdge* Staff

How to Get Started With Modems
By Jim Kimble

How to Understand and Buy Computers
By Dan Gookin

How to Understand and Find Software
By Wally Wang

Parent's Guide to Educational Software and Computers
By Lynn Stewart and Toni Michael

Ten (& More) Interesting Uses for Your Home Computer
By Tina Berke